Louisiana

"Scattered to the Wind"
Dispersal and Wanderings
of the Acadians, 1755-1809

With my best regards,

Carl A. Brasseaux

4/24/92

by Carl A. Brasseaux

Published by
The Center for Louisiana Studies
University of Southwestern Louisiana

To Steve, Kelree, Lauren,
Calvin, Sharon, Courtney, Andrew,
and Evan

The title is taken from
Alfred, Lord Tennyson, *The Two Voices*, stanza 11.

The cover illustration represents
an artist's conception of the Acadian deportation from Grand Pré.
Courtesy Parks Canada.

Library of Congress Catalog Number: 91-72563
ISBN Number: 0-940984-70-9

University of Southwestern Louisiana
Lafayette, Louisiana

CONTENTS

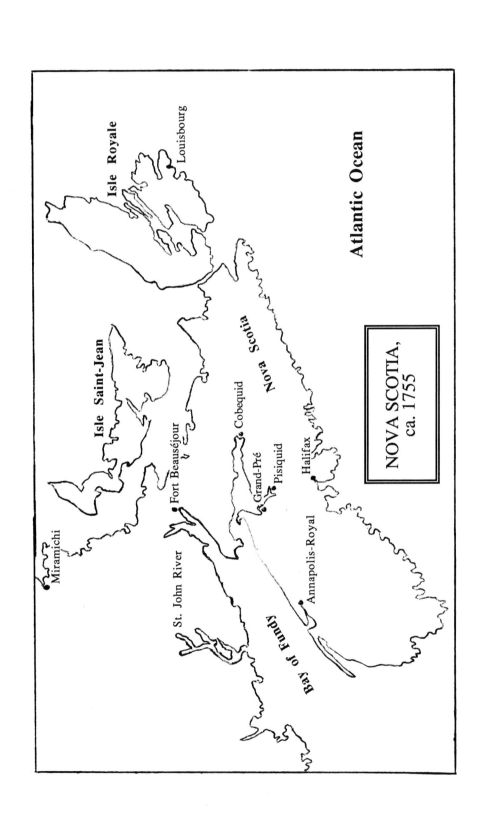

Isle Royale

Louisbourg

Atlantic Ocean

Isle Saint-Jean

Nova Scotia

Cobequid

Fort Beauséjour

Grand-Pré
Pisiquid

Halifax

Miramichi

St. John River

Annapolis-Royal

Bay of Fundy

NOVA SCOTIA,
ca. 1755

"Scattered to the Wind"
Dispersal and Wanderings of the Acadians, 1755-1809*

Impact of the Grand Dérangement

The dispersal of the Acadian population—perhaps better known to historians as the *Grand Dérangement*—is unquestionably the pivotal event in Acadian history. Longfellow attempted to portray the tragic consequences of the deportation of the Acadian population from the Bay of Fundy Basin through his epic *Evangeline,* but the narrow focus of this work failed to convey the magnitude of the disruption and misery upon the Acadian population. To fully comprehend the impact of this event upon the Acadian community, one need merely examine its demographic repercussions. There are presently, by the most liberal estimates, 1,500,000 Acadians scattered about two continents; the actual figure, however, is probably closer to 700,000, for figures in Louisiana and the Canadian Maritimes have been inflated in recent years for political reasons.[1] Had the *Grand Dérangement* never taken place and if the pre-dispersal population growth rate of 100 percent every twenty-to-twenty-five years had remained constant over the next two centuries, the Acadian population in 1975 would have numbered approximately 7,680,000.[2] (See below, Table I.)

The Grand Dérangement

The *Grand Dérangement* resulted in large part from the Acadian refusal to become a party to the almost continuous Anglo-French imperial wars in North America during the eighteenth century. The colony of Acadia changed hands—either through conquest or diplomatic negotiations—ten times between 1604 and 1710, when the British assumed permanent control of the region and renamed it Nova Scotia. Because of the frequent changes in European domination of the colony, the colonists consciously strove to avoid the potentially murderous crossfire that future colonial clashes would inevitably bring.

The local Micmac Indians, whose numbers, in the early eighteenth century, matched those of the Acadians, were staunch allies of the French, and Acadians feared reprisals if they aligned themselves with their new British overlords.

TABLE I

PROJECTED ACADIAN GROWTH RATES, 1750-1975

Year	Population
1750	15,000(?)
1775	30,000
1800	60,000
1825	120,000
1850	240,000
1875	480,000
1900	960,000
1925	1,920,000
1950	3,840,000
1975	7,680,000

The British, who were always greatly outnumbered by their reluctant Acadian subjects, consequently maintained a very tenuous hold over the colony and were thus extremely anxious to bring the Acadians into their camp through an ironclad oath of allegiance. Only in 1730 did the Acadians finally acquiesce, and then only after verbal (though unauthorized and quite spurious) assurances from the colonial governor—known as the "conventions of 1730"—that the Acadians would enjoy neutral status in future Anglo-French confrontations.

Over the next two decades, the Acadians honored their commitment to neutrality during inter-colonial warfare despite French-Canadian attempts to incite Bay of Fundy area settlers to revolt. British officials nevertheless remained uneasy about their Acadian subjects, particularly after 1750, when a French Catholic missionary ordered his Micmac parishioners to burn a large Acadian village in order to force its inhabitants into French-held territory and ultimately into the local French militia. The British colonial government responded to this external threat by attempting to extract, once again, an unconditional oath of allegiance from Nova Scotia's now extensive Acadian population. Still unwilling to be caught in a crossfire, the Acadians refused British demands and insisted that they would in no way alter the terms of the 1730 conventions.[3]

By unswerving adherence to the "conventions of 1730," the Acadians in 1750 had foiled a British effort to undermine their semiautonomous position in the colony. Unqualified subservience to the British colonial regime, many contemporary British observers and many students of the Acadian diaspora agree, was the first step in an evolving British plan for assimilating the potentially subversive, French-speaking Catholics into the Anglo-Protestant mainstream of the British empire. This eventuality was well understood by the Acadian leadership. Thus, though their struggle against the colonial regime was couched in political terms, the Acadians were actually fighting for their cultural survival. The Acadians were given a brief reprieve during the administration of the conciliatory Peregrine Hopson, but the growing border tensions between the French and English North American empires embroiled them once again in a power struggle with the government, now centered in Halifax.[4]

Suspicious of Acadian motives and no longer dependent upon the good graces of the French-speaking community for its survival, the ruling English oligarchy was now resolved to settle the festering Acadian problem once and for all. The fate of the Acadian population lay with the Nova Scotian governor and colonial council, in whose hands all authority was vested by the colonial charter. The chief executive, however, played a pivotal role in shaping the British response to the recently resurrected Acadian problem. In 1754, Major Charles Lawrence succeeded Hopson as governor of Nova Scotia. A professional soldier who had most recently served on Nova Scotia's western border strengthening the colony's defenses against the growing French military threat, Lawrence was preoccupied with the vulnerability of the colony he now commanded. And, in Lawrence's mind, the internal threat posed by the Acadians was quite as formidable as that posed by the French fortresses that now occupied strategic points on the colony's flanks. The colonial defense demanded that Nova Scotia mobilize all of its resources, a task virtually impossible in the face of the at least passive (and possibly active) resistance of the colony's large Acadian majority. Thus Lawrence was most anxious to secure an unqualified oath of allegiance from the Acadians, but, unlike his predecessor, Lawrence would brook absolutely no opposition.[5]

The Acadians, on the other hand, saw no reason to alter their traditional demand for neutrality. And, as their population, which now numbered between 12,000 and 18,000 individuals (exact figures are unavailable because the last comprehensive, pre-dispersal census was taken in 1714),[6] easily dwarfed its English counterpart, despite the establishment of Halifax, the French-speakers did not feel intimidated. Failing to perceive the growing desperation of Lawrence and other key members of the British colonial administration, the Acadians exhibited no interest whatsoever in voluntarily linking their destinies with those of the British empire. In 1750, the Acadians had witnessed with horror the fiery destruction of the Beaubassin district by the Micmac Indians and the increasing belligerence of the French forces along Nova Scotia's borders augured ill for anyone in the British camp.

TABLE II

ACADIAN POPULATION GROWTH, 1654-1755

Year	Total
1654	300-350
1701	1450
1737	7598
1755	12000-18000[7]

The Acadian problem, as always, held the promise of long duration, especially as Lawrence lacked the means and a legal motive for driving from Nova Scotia thousands of French-speakers who, by virtue of the "conventions of 1730," were at least nominally British subjects. Nevertheless, as early as November 1754, Lawrence conspired with Massachusetts

Governor William Shirley, commander-in-chief of British forces in New England and an outspoken proponent of English colonial supremacy in North America, for the unauthorized deportation of Acadians from Nova Scotia. False rumors (possibly initiated by Lawrence and Shirley or their agents) provided the conspirators with a pretext for massing British troops in Nova Scotia. In late spring 1755, 1,800 British soldiers from New England sailed to the Isthmus of Chignecto. Meanwhile, Lawrence coerced the Acadians into surrendering their firearms. Now largely defenseless, the Acadians became easy prey for the pro-deportation administrators, particularly following the British capture of French Fort Beauséjour in June, 1755, which sealed off the only overland escape route to the mainland. Deprived of their weapons and barred from escape, the Acadians were completely at the mercy of their British overlords.[8]

Lawrence was quick to exploit this advantage. In late June, 1755, he ordered all Acadian settlements in Nova Scotia to send delegates to the colonial capital ostensibly to discuss the possible return of confiscated Acadian firearms. When the delegation representing the Mines area—the most thickly populated Acadian settlements in the Bay of Fundy Basin appeared before the governor on July 3, however, Lawrence demanded that they accept, on behalf of their constituents, an unconditional oath of allegiance to Britain. The Acadian delegates stubbornly refused to concede their neutral status and consequently were summarily imprisoned to serve as an example to their equally recalcitrant constituents.

The refusal of the Mines delegation to cave in to Lawrence's demand created a crisis of authority within the colony, a crisis exacerbated by the arrival on July 23 of reports of General Edward Braddock's humiliating defeat by a motley French and Indian force in the middle Atlantic colonies. From the perspective of the British colonial administration, another colonial war was imminent, and Nova Scotia's French-speaking population, through its rejection of the foregoing oath, was telegraphing its intention of becoming a francophile fifth column. Thus, following Lawrence's lead, the colonial council, which had recently ordered all Acadians in Nova Scotia to take an unconditional oath of allegiance, on July 31 ordered the forcible removal of the colony's large Acadian population.[9]

To effect the removal as expeditiously and as cheaply as possible, Lawrence devised a scheme for assuring the Acadians' peaceable submission to deportation. Drawing upon engineer Charles Morris' memorandum on Acadian deportation, Charles Lawrence directed the English commandants at Beaubassin, Pisiquid, and Annapolis-Royal to lure the local Acadian males into their respective ports. There, the unsuspecting victims would be arrested and detained until the arrival of transports which would carry them into exile. The detention of male hostages would ensure that the local women and children would remain home with their possessions and livestock, thus expediting their removal from the colony. Finally, all Acadian property would be confiscated to reimburse the English government for the cost of their removal, while all Acadian homes and boats would be destroyed.[10]

This plan was executed with ruthless precision by the British commanders in the Beaubassin and Pisiquid/Mines areas. At Fort Cumberland (formerly French Fort Beauséjour at Beaubassin) on August 9, 1755, Colonel Robert Monckton's force captured 250 to 400 local Acadians summoned to the post ostensibly for an important gubernatorial decree regarding their lands. The effective use of subterfuge and the element of surprise also permitted the British military to arrest and detain 418 Acadian men and teenagers at the Grand Pré church on September 5. In both communities, the wives and children of the detainees were notified of the loved ones' arrest and ordered to prepare for their imminent deportation from their home district. On the day appointed for their removal—usually five days after the detention of the local Acadian men—the deportees were divided into groups by age and by sex and then marched to nearby landings. There, they were placed in longboats and distributed among waiting British merchant vessels anchored in the Bay of Fundy.[11]

The settlers adjoining Grand Pré and its dependencies were demoralized by the removal of the Grand Pré settlers and were intimidated by the presence of large British military patrols in their area. Residents of these settlements consequently offered no resistance to subsequent deportation efforts. By mid-October, 1755, most of the Acadians had been forcibly removed from the heavily populated Minas Basin area of Nova Scotia.[12]

Winslow's efficiency in uprooting the Grand Pré and Beaubassin Acadians contrasts sharply with the incompetence of Major John Handfield, sent by Lawrence to eradicate the Acadian population in the Annapolis-Royal area. Apparently unable to lie convincingly, Handfield was unable to lure the local Acadian males into a snare similar to those used effectively at Beaubassin and Grand Pré. Indeed, suspecting a trap, the local Acadians fled into the woods, where they remained in hiding for several weeks. The onset of the Canadian winter, however, forced the refugees to surrender in early November and, by early December, 1755, 1,664 Acadian residents of the former colonial capital and its environs had boarded British transport vessels.[13]

The Acadians taken prisoner at Annapolis-Royal, Grand Pré and its environs, and Beaubassin numbered approximately 5,400 individuals. Deportations continued on a smaller scale in succeeding years, and by 1760, according to Andrew Hill Clark, approximately 6,000 Acadians had been sent into exile.

TABLE III

ACADIAN DEPORTEES, 1755-1760[14]

District	Number	
Grand Pré	2182	
Annapolis	1664	
Pisiquid	1100	(approximate)
Beaubassin	1100	(approximate)
Total	6050	(approximate)

These Acadians were distributed among the British seaboard colonies—from Georgia to Massachusetts—and England. Those deemed the most dangerous Acadians—those who had previously been French conscripts at Fort Beauséjour—were sent to those seaboard provinces farthest from their native land, while the farmers of Pisiquid, Grand Pré and Annapolis-Royal were widely distributed throughout the lower thirteen colonies.

TABLE IV
DISTRIBUTION OF ACADIAN EXILES, 1755

Colony	Number
Georgia	400
S. Carolina	942
N. Carolina	50
Virginia	1500
Maryland	913
Pennsylvania	454
New York	344
Connecticut	731
Massachusetts	735
Bound for N.C. but escaped	232
Total	6301

TABLE V
ACADIANS IN EXILE, 1763[15]

Massachusetts	1043
Connecticut	666
New York	249
Maryland	810
Pennsylvania	383
South Carolina	280
Georgia	185
Nova Scotia	1249
St. John River Valley, N.B.	87
England	866
France	3400
Quebec	2000
Prince Edward Island	300
Baie des Chaleurs	700

Acadians in Exile

Crammed into the dank, dark holds of their small British transports, given substandard food and water, and denied knowledge of their destination, the Acadian deportees were a miserable lot indeed. As the Acadians exiled to Pennsylvania subsequently recalled: "we were so crowded on the transport vessels, that we had not room even for all our bodies to lay down at once, and consequently were prevented from carrying with us proper necessities." This statement is amply supported by extant documentation revealing that most of the British transports carried approximately one-third more passengers than they were designed to hold, resulting in rapid depletion of the ships' stores. The detrimental effects of overcrowding and poor diet had devastating effects upon the formerly robust health of the exiles. The general decline in the exiles' state of physical wellbeing was exacerbated by the detrimental effects of stress and seasickness produced by the storms and heavy seas that plagued the crossing. It is thus hardly surprising that, almost without exception, epidemics (usually typhus and smallpox) broke out among the exiles either during the crossing or upon their arrival at an English colonial seaport.[16]

These epidemics did little to ingratiate the exiles with their reluctant hosts. The Acadian exiles arrived unannounced at the colonial seaports designated as their destinations by Charles Lawrence, and the stunned colonial officials in these "host" communities were understandably wary of their destitute and decidedly hostile Acadian charges. Lacking instructions from British imperial authorities regarding disposition of the exiles, officials in the seaboard colonies consistently treated their Acadian wards as potential fifth columnists. For months before the first exiles appeared in their harbors, colonial newspapers had been filled with anti-French propaganda, much of which had been directed specifically against Nova Scotia's Acadian population. The Acadians—whose numbers were inflated to 30,000 by British propagandists—were depicted as immoral "papists" who occupied the best farmland on the northern Atlantic coastline, land that God had clearly intended for proper English Protestants. Though nominally British subjects, these

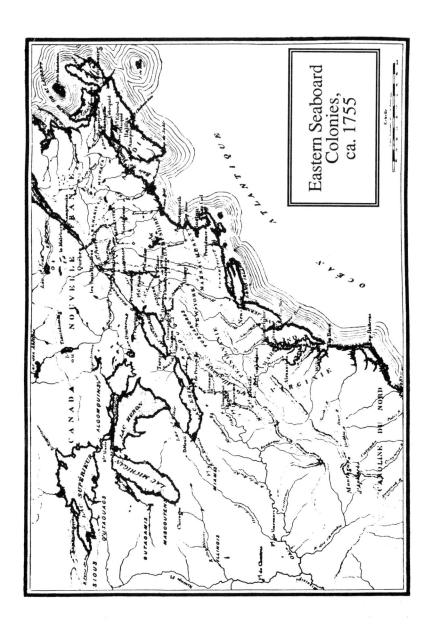

Eastern Seaboard
Colonies,
ca. 1755

papists were fully expected to join their co-religionists, the French, and their fierce Indian allies in the impending intercolonial struggle for North American domination. As the French were then threatening British frontier positions all along the Appalachian Mountains, the Acadians, in the view of the British colonial administrators, would constitute, even in exile, a formidable fifth column, capable perhaps of inciting servile insurrections in the slave colonies to aid the French cause. The long-term threat to internal security posed by the Acadians was, of course, immediately overshadowed by the threat of infection that they posed to the established colonial populations and the financial burden which their resettlement would entail.[17]

Virginia

Unwilling to be saddled with these myriad problems, Virginia flatly refused to accept the 1,500 Acadian exiles entrusted to its care. These Acadians were summarily dispatched to England (at Virginia's expense), where they remained in coastal detention centers for the duration of the Seven Years War. (See England, below.)

Georgia

The Old Dominion's southern neighbors were equally inhospitable. The governor of Georgia, John Reynolds, rejected his colony's allotment of human cargo when the first transport cast anchor off Savannah in early December, 1755. Indeed, before leaving for a series of meetings with Southeastern Indians, Reynolds forbade the colony's chief pilot "at his peril to bring any more such people into the Province." The governor's orders, however, were ignored and nearly 400 exiles were deposited on Georgia's shores. Because of the circumstances of their arrival, the destitute Acadians were generally ignored by the colonial government for the first year of their exile in the former penal colony. In fact, only when they petitioned the colonial government for emergency assistance in January 1756 were they recognized at all, and then only to the extent that those exiles too ill to support themselves were given a week's supply of rice.

The government's benign neglect of the Georgia Acadians provided them the independence to coordinate their escape from the southernmost British seaboard colony, and, by early spring 1756, they had secured—apparently with the Governor Reynold's assistance—ten small sailing vessels. Sometime before the beginning of March, 1756, the Acadians began coasting northward, with the intention of ultimately returning to Nova Scotia. Despite the wretched conditions aboard these open vessels (most of which were only marginally seaworthy) and despite inducements to settle by officials in present-day North Carolina, this determined band of Acadians pressed steadily onward. Only ninety individuals, less that half of the 200 original voyagers, aboard seven boats reached Massachusetts Bay in July, 1756, and there they were arrested and detained by British authorities who feared the consequences of their return to Nova Scotia.[18]

Some of the few Acadians remaining in Georgia developed skills required by the local plantation and shipping industries. The oars and pikes that they manufactured were even reportedly exported to the West Indies. Most of the remaining Acadians, however, remained mired in dire poverty. Thus lacking the resources to leave, they appear to have remained in the Georgia coastal region until the 1763 Treaty of Paris ended the fighting between England and France and extended to the exiles an eighteen-month grace period in which to relocate on French soil. Most of the surviving Georgia Acadians appear to have used this opportunity to migrate to French Saint-Domingue (present-day Haiti).[19]

South Carolina

The Acadian experience in Georgia was repeated in neighboring South Carolina, where 942 exiles arrived between November 1755 and late January 1756. South Carolina, populated primarily with the descendants of Huguenots exiled from France half a century earlier, was extremely distressed by the arrival of hundreds of "bigoted Papists." The Acadians were fully expected either to incite to rebellion the local slave population which already outnumbered whites by a two-to-one margin or to lead to victory neighboring, French-allied Indians. The fears of the South Carolinians seemed abundantly justified by the unbridled animosity and "impudence" of the exiles toward their captors. An unidentified South Carolinian noted that "they are insolent Rascals, [who] talk in a high strain, calling themselves Subjects of the French King, own they were Neutrals, and that they took up Arms against us. . . . They say they'll settle here, if we'll allow them such Privileges with their Priests. . . . They will not even upon any Terms take the Oaths of Allegiance—By this we may judge what a pernicious dangerous Gang they were in Nova Scotia."[20]

Hundreds of Acadians were consequently forced to remain aboard their overcrowded transports for nearly one month while reluctant hosts decided what to do with them. When health conditions became such that the colonial government was finally forced to allow the exiles to land, the exiles were herded together along the beaches, where they were evidently encouraged to leave the colony aboard merchant vessels bound for England. The government, meanwhile, demonstrated no determination to resolve the festering Acadian question, and, unwilling to endure any longer the uncertainty clouding their future, large groups of exiles attempted to escape into the North American interior on at least three occasions within two months of their arrival. Fearing that they would join hostile Indians there, the South Carolina government mobilized posses to pursue and return the first two bands of fugitives. Only thirty Acadians managed to escape; their fate is unknown. The third attempt was somewhat more successful. A small band of undetermined size escaped from its detention camp, made its way to the Santee River Valley where its members stole goods, arms and ammunition from a local plantation, and set out in search for Fort Duquesne, the French stronghold in the Ohio Valley. Only two Acadians are known to have completed the trek.[21]

The Acadian desire to leave South Carolina matched that of the native South Carolinians who desperately wanted them to leave. Consequently, during its April, 1756, session, the

colonial assembly authorized public subscriptions in the amount
of 12,000 pounds, with all contributions dedicated to the purchase
and outfitting of two ships which would provide the exiles
passage out of the colony. The local citizenry quickly raised the
necessary funds, and two "ancient" vessels and "a small
quantity of bad provisions" were purchased and proferred to the
Acadians. Though anxious to leave, the exiles were fully
cognizant of the dangers in sailing unfamiliar waters.
Sensing the South Carolinians' sense of desperation, the
Acadians thus demanded that the colonial government provide
pilots before they would agree to leave. This request was
summarily rejected, for, though the South Carolinians fully
expected the Acadians to return to the Bay of Fundy area, the
hiring of two pilots for this voyage would have constituted an
official endorsement of their repatriation and the inevitable
wrath of the British administration.[22]

Conceding the point, an undetermined, but large number of
South Carolina Acadians boarded the two proferred ships and
immediately set sail for Nova Scotia. Their vessels shipped so
much water, however, that they were obliged to beach them near
Hampton, Virginia. The Virginians near the landing site were
quite as intimidated by the Acadian presence as had been the
South Carolinians. They therefore permitted the exiles to pool
their resources—400 Spanish *piastres*—to purchase a vessel and
continue their odyssey.[23]

This ship, however, proved quite as unseaworthy as its two
precedessors, and the Acadians were forced to beach it
somewhere along Maryland's Atlantic coast. For two months,
the makeshift Acadian crew labored to repair the "wreck".
They ultimately succeeded in making the vessel seaworthy, and
again set sail for the Bay of Fundy. Fortune smiled more
kindly upon the Acadians during this voyage, and they
eventually made their way to the St. John River, in present-day
Nova Scotia. Upon debarkation, many of the male survivors
joined Lt. Charles des Champs de Boishébert's small French
force and subsequently waged guerilla warfare against the
British in Nova Scotia.[24]

The courageous example of these voyagers remained a
powerful example to those Acadians who remained in exile in

the southern Atlantic colonies. In both Georgia and South Carolina, the remaining Acadians, particularly those who had difficulty in finding gainful employment, were forcibly distributed throughout the coastal counties. Families were divided, and teenaged males were bound out to planters as indentured farm laborers (thereby giving rise to the unfounded legend that Acadians here were sold into slavery) or, less commonly, apprenticed to artisans. In many instances, indentured Acadians had to be bound in irons and forcibly removed from their families. Such cruelty provided the catalyst that drove almost all of the remaining Acadians from South Carolina and Georgia. The evidence suggests that of those who survived the onslaught of smallpox and other epidemic diseases in the aftermath of their arrival, many eventually congregated in the coastal settlements from which they surreptitiously sailed for the Bay of Fundy area or for the French colony of Saint-Domingue.[25]

Maryland and Pennsylvania

The Middle Atlantic Colonies, unlike their southern counterparts, maintained strict control over their Acadian populations, perhaps because they felt more directly threatened by French and Indian forces to the west. Thus lacking mobility, the Acadian exiles in these colonies were completely at the mercy of their Anglo-American custodians. In view of Maryland's origins as a refuge for persecuted English Catholics and neighboring Pennsylvania's beginnings as a Quaker colony, one would expect the Acadian experience here to have been relatively mild, and, indeed, it has been depicted as such by Anglophile historians. Yet, this chapter of the Acadian diaspora is among the bleakest of many dark episodes along North America's Atlantic Coast.

The first Acadian exiles arrived at Annapolis, Maryland, the provincial capital, sometime between September 20 and 30, 1755. The 913 exiles, packed aboard four dreadfully overcrowded transport vessels, had consumed all of their allotted provisions en route, and thus the host community was compelled to provide immediate support for their unexpected guests. The burden thus imposed upon the colonial capital's population occasioned considerable grumbling from both the general population and the local press, and, as a consequence, an emergency meeting of the Provincial Council was convoked to partition the exiles among the Maryland counties. One of the transports was subsequently dispatched to the Patuxent River, a second to the Wicomico River, a third to the Choptank River, and the fourth, the *Leopard*, was directed to remain at the provincial capital.[26]

Upon reaching their destinations within Maryland, the Acadians found themselves in rather unenviable circumstances. As nominal British subjects, they were not entitled to any particular assistance from the provincial or local governments, and as French-speaking Catholics in a region that was at war with French Catholics, they were shunned, feared, and reviled by the region's Anglo-Protestant majority. Native Catholics were legally enjoined from assisting their co-religionists. Some assistance was provided by a few philanthropic individuals—often by those who had previously been most vocal in their support of the proposed Acadian expulsion. Because of the broad range of basic services required by the exiles and the correspondingly heavy financial burden which they entailed, these good samaritans were soon compelled to abandon their wards. Fully cognizant of the incompatability between their job skills and those required by the Maryland economy, the Acadians demanded that the government recognize their status as prisoners of war and accordingly provide food and shelter for them. The government, however, rejected this claim, indicating that the Acadians had acquired full British citizenship through the "conventions of 1730." Consequently, at least one group of Acadians was literally forced to exist, without shelter, in the frozen, snow-covered countryside, huddling together for warmth, for several days before adequate shelter could be found. Forced to make their own way in the world, the Acadians grudgingly accepted the low-paying and often degrading jobs offered by their reluctant hosts and gradually improved their lot, though never rising above the poverty level.[27]

While unable to provide economic assistance to the

Acadians because of their British citizenship, the provincial government paradoxically treated the exiles as prisoners, adopting regulations to restrict their individual liberties and freedom of movement in early 1756. At Governor Horatio Sharpe's urging, the provincial legislature adopted, on April 23, 1756, "An Act to Empower the Justice of the Several County Courts, to Make Provision for the Late Inhabitants of Nova Scotia, and for Regulating Their Conduct." The bill, reflecting the prevailing public revulsion, fear and suspicion of the French-Catholic immigrants, required the exiles, which were characterized as indolent and obstinate, to "rely upon their own Labour and Industry to procure a comfortable subsistence for themselves." In cases where Acadian parents appeared either unable or unwilling to support adequately their children, the county magistrates were empowered to "bind out" Acadian children "upon the best terms they could make" (vis-à-vis the provincial government) with local artisans, planters, or businessmen. All unemployed, but able-bodied Acadians were to be deemed vagrants and were to be jailed until they manifested an interest in finding employment. To ensure that employment was indeed available, the number of Acadians exceeding the local labor demand were to be transferred to neighboring counties where there was less surplus labor.[28]

The act also furnished the magistrates with administrative machinery for preventing the exiles from reaching the colony's vulnerable western border, where British troops were under orders to shoot the Acadians on sight. All Acadians wishing to travel more than ten miles from their residence were required to secure a passport from the local justice of the peace. Violators were subject to citizens' arrests, five-day imprisonment, and subsequent, forcible removal to the prisoner's abode.[29]

The Acadians' freedom of movement was further restricted by Maryland's militia restrictions. Through "An Act for Regulating the Militia of the Province of Maryland," enacted on May 22, 1756, the Acadian exiles were banned from attending militia training sessions; failure to comply with the prohibition would inevitably result in detention "out of View of the Said Place of Training until sun set that day."[30]

During the two years in which they were enforced (1756-

1758), the anti-Acadian acts effectively reduced Acadian mobility, and, in late August 1756, Horatio Sharpe could assure his counterpart in Nova Scotia, Charles Lawrence, that "None of the French who were imported into this Province have been suffered either by Land or Water to return . . . thither [Nova Scotia]."[31]

Though confined to their host province for the duration of the Seven Years' War and though oppressed by their host government, the Acadian community bent under the pressures brought to bear against it, but it did not break. Throughout the conflict, the Acadians openly supported the French cause and took no pains to conceal their delight at French military victories. Such successes, however, became more and more infrequent as the war progressed. France's ultimate defeat, which also dashed their lingering hopes of repatriation to Nova Scotia, hung like a pall over Maryland's Acadian community in the 1760s.[32]

Repatriation had symbolized liberation from the dreadful conditions under which the Acadian population existed in Maryland. Victims of malnutrition and epidemic diseases, Maryland's Acadian community had actually declined by twenty-seven percent (913 to 667) between 1755 and 1763. Mired in poverty, many exiles could not afford adequate housing or food. Widows generally survived by begging from door to door. Such activities produced a sharply negative backlash among native Marylanders who were taxed to support those Acadians who could not support themselves. Thus, by the mid-1760s, the surviving Acadians desperately longed for an opportunity to leave the site of their captivity, while the native Marylanders were equally anxious to see them leave. Thus, in the late 1760s, most of the Maryland Acadians, responding to invitations to migrate to Louisiana from friends and relatives newly established in the Spanish colony's Attakapas District, pooled their resources, chartered ships, and sailed to the Mississippi Valley. Those burdened with large families, particularly widows, often joined the exodus by virtue of subsidies granted by local governmental bodies.[33]

The Maryland Acadians were joined in their trek to Louisiana by most of the surviving Acadians in Pennsylvania.

The Acadian experience in the Quaker colony bears a striking parallel to that of the exiles in neighboring Maryland. The 454 Acadians who arrived in the Delaware River before Philadelphia between November 18 and 20, 1755, became the scapegoats for the colony's raging francophobia, resulting from successful French and Indian raids on the Keystone colony's western borders. These popular fears were soon translated into action by Pennsylvania Governor Robert H. Morris, who placed the exiles under armed guard aboard the three vessels (the *Hannah, Three Friends,* and *Swan*) upon which they had sailed from Nova Scotia. He then detained a large contingent of provincial militia in Philadelphia to protect the colonial capital from the perceived (but non-existant) military threat posed by the unarmed exiles.[34]

While thus detained aboard the overcrowded vessels, the Acadian exiles succumbed to various epidemic diseases. These diseases posed a real threat to Philadelphia and spurred the provincial government into further negative actions. At Morris' suggestion, the Acadians were quarantined on Province Island—at public expense—until the ravages of these diseases abated. Only after the threat of contamination had subsided, did the Pennsylvania legislature seriously consider the long-term disposition of the exiles. Legislation signed into law on March 5, 1756, named four prominent Philadelphia Huguenots sympathetic to the plight of the Acadians to a commission to coordinate the dispersal of the exiles throughout the easternmost Pennsylvania provinces. These commissioners were to place one Acadian per county township, provided that the township wardens of the poor accepted them. The commissioners would also rent land for Acadian farmers, who were to be given a maximum of ten pounds' worth of agricultural implements to help them support themselves. Widows, orphans, and other exiles incapable of supporting themselves were to be placed on the dole. All of these expenses were to be supported by the provincial war chest.[35]

The foregoing act was to remain in force for one year, at the expiration of which the Acadian exiles would presumably have been self-sufficient. The theoretical base upon which it was conceived was sound, but the legislation failed miserably in practice. Most rural townships, in which the Acadian agriculturists could conceivably have found a new life, refused to accept the exiles who were almost universally viewed as a potential fifth column. Meanwhile, the Acadians themselves refused to be dispersed, for they fully understood that such dilution of their numbers would inevitably result in their assimilation by the Anglo-Protestant majority. The exiles thus congregated in Philadelphia's slums, where they remained on the government dole for the duration of the Acadian dispersal act.[36]

When government support of the exiles ceased in September, 1756, the Acadian leaders in Philadelphia demanded permission to leave Pennsylvania, noting that they lacked the means of supporting themselves and preferred to die in their native land. The Acadian remonstrance concluded on a defiant note, stating "we shall never freely consent to settle in this province."[37]

The Pennsylvania government, which smuggly assumed that the Acadian problem had been resolved, was jolted from its complacency by the unanticipated protest against the suspension of the dole. The Acadian protest elicited an angry response from Pennsylvania politicians, who railed against the exiles' claim to prisoner-of-war status and who called for their forcible dispersal among the province's easternmost counties. Cooler heads prevailed, however, and Quaker William Griffith persuaded the legislature that the Acadian outburst had been prompted by their wretched economic circumstances. According to Griffith, most of Pennsylvania's Acadians had been refused employment by bigoted Philadelphia businessmen. Able-bodied Acadians had responded by making wooden shoes and fabricating cloth from discarded rags in an attempt to support themselves, but, as no market existed for these commodities in the colonial capital, they had no means of supporting themselves. Acting out of frustration and desperation, many Acadians had resorted to petty thievery to support themselves and their families. Many exiles nevertheless lived on an inadequate diet which included "neither meat nor bread." They thus fell victim to various epidemic diseases which decimated their numbers.[38]

Persuaded of the exiles' plight by Griffith, the Pennsylvania legislature sought to resolve the festering Acadian problem once and for all. In January 1757, the assembly passed a bill, signed into law on January 18, that required Acadian parents to apprentice their children to Anglo-American artisans to ensure their support. These children would be educated in the English language. Aged, infirm and handicapped Acadians, on the other hand, would be supported by the government.[39]

The Acadians loudly protested this heavy-handed effort to destroy their families and to assimilate forcibly their children into the dominant culture. Demanding to know whether they were "subjects, prisoners, slaves, or freemen," Philadelphia Acadians again sought permission to leave the Keystone Colony, offering to sell their meagre personal possessions to secure passage to another colony. The Pennsylvania government officially ignored these protests, but made no move to enforce the foregoing legislation.[40]

Such governmental inertia, however, was counterproductive, for it drove the Acadians to desperation. Many Acadian men publicly proclaimed their desire to abandon their wives and children and to join the French forces to the west in their war against the Anglo-Pennsylvanians. Their "mutinous" spirit was sufficiently disruptive to attract the attention of Lord Loudoun, commander-in-chief of British forces in North America who ordered the arrest of several prominent Acadians to subdue the exiles. The Acadians responded with a remonstrance in French setting forth their grievances. Loudoun "returned it and said [he] could receive no memorial from the King's subjects but in English, on which they [the Acadians] had a general meeting at which they determined they would give no Memorial but in French". Infuriated by the Acadian response, Loudoun ordered the incarcerated Acadian leaders placed aboard the H. M. S. *Sutherland,* a British warship bound for England.[41]

Though these Acadian prisoners were subsequently acquitted, released, and returned to Philadelphia, their absence deprived the exiles of their spokesmen. The Acadians nevertheless remained notoriously intransigent and insolent—

from the Anglo-Protestant viewpoint—resisting renewed government efforts in 1761 to "bind out" their children and petitioning King George in 1760 to redress their grievances against the Pennsylvania government. In 1763, they notified the French crown of their desire to migrate to France and, when that avenue of escape did not materialize, many Pennsylvania Acadians accepted the Comte d'Estaing's 1764 invitation to migrate to Saint-Domingue. Used as forced laborers by the French government and forced to carve a naval base from the jungles along the island's northern coast, most of these refugees died of tropical fevers, while their children perished from malnutrition and scurvy. Most of the Pennsylvania Acadians, however, remained in and around Philadelphia until the late 1760s, when they joined their relatives and friends exiled to neighboring Maryland in a massive migration to Louisiana.[42]

New York

The misery of the Acadians exiled to the Middle Atlantic Colonies was shared by their countrymen sent to New York and Connecticut. Unlike neighboring New Jersey, which refused to accept any of the exiles, New York reluctantly opened its doors to three contingents of Acadians. The first, consisting of an undetermined number of Cape Sable Acadians, arrived aboard a schooner on April 28, 1756. Two hundred additional Acadians reached New York harbor aboard the *Experiment* the following May 6. These exiles were the survivors of the ship's original complement of 250 Annapolis Royal Acadians. Setting out from Nova Scotia in December 1755, they were carried by a powerful winter storm to Antigua. Here several Acadians escaped their captors and made their way to the French Antilles. The remaining captives, however, were forced to continue the five-month voyage to New York, and reportedly arrived there "poor, naked and destitute of every convenience." The third contingent of Acadians came from Georgia en route to Nova Scotia and were detained by New York's governor upon reaching Long Island on August 22, 1756.[43]

New York looked to the Middle Atlantic Colonies for guidance in dealing with its Acadian wards. In July 1756, the colonial assembly adopted legislation patterned upon Maryland's "Act to Empower the Justice of the Several County Courts." Unlike the Middle Atlantic Colonies, however, New York successfully implemented its statutory regulations instituted against the Acadian population. The exiles were distributed throughout those New York counties farthest from French Canada—those on Long Island and Staten Island. In addition, at least 110 of the 344 Acadians (32 percent) known to have lived in exile in New York were indentured to Anglo-Americans in late August 1756. A significant, but undetermined number of the Acadians thus indentured rebelled against forcible separation from their families by bolting for French Canada in 1757; most of the fugitives, however, were subsequently captured and imprisoned. The abortive escape attempt seems to have quelled further resistance, and the New York Acadians quietly endured captivity until the Treaty of Paris afforded them an opportunity to leave. Most of these exiles appear to have migrated to Saint-Domingue, where they shared the fate of their ill-starred confrères from Pennsylvania; an additional twenty New York Acadians made their way to Louisiana via Mobile in early 1764.[44]

Connecticut

The attempt by the New York government to regiment the Acadian population pales by comparison to that of Connecticut. Believing that the security of New England hinged upon that of Nova Scotia, the Connecticut legislature, in November 1755—months before the arrival of the first Acadians—passed a resolution authorizing the colonial governor to take all steps necessary to dispose of any French Neutrals sent there for detention. Acting under this mandate, Governor Thomas Fitch convoked the legislature into emergency session upon the arrival of the first contingent of Acadians and, under his guidance, bills were enacted to distribute the anticipated influx of exiles among fifty designated towns. The legislation also directed the "selectmen" [aldermen] of each town to maintain the integrity of nuclear families in partitioning the anticipated waves of exiled immigrants. These local officials were also to provide public assistance to indigent and handicapped Acadians and to maintain strict controls over their able-bodied confrères to prevent them from departing their designated host communities and congregating into larger, potentially dangerous groups.[45]

The first Acadians thus distributed arrived at New London aboard the *Elizabeth* on January 21, 1756. These 277 exiles from Annapolis-Royal were followed the next day by 173 more Acadians from the Minas Basin area (Mines, Grand Pré, Pisiquid) aboard an unidentified schooner. In May 1756, 260 Acadians reached Connecticut aboard the *Edward* which, like the *Experiment* destined for New York, had been driven to Antigua by a hurricane-force winter storm. There, the Acadians apparently contracted smallpox, and this disease decimated the exiles during their subsequent passage to New London.[46]

Upon arrival, the Acadian immigrants were distributed throughout Connecticut in conformity with the foregoing legislation. Little is known of their subsequent activities other than the fact that their movements were severely restricted. But it is nevertheless obvious that the exiles were extremely dissatisfied with the conditions under which they lived in Connecticut, for in 1763, 666 Acadians (91 percent of the Acadians known to have been sent to that colony and apparently all of the survivors) there petitioned the French king for transportation to France. When French assistance failed to materialize, some of the disgruntled Connecticut Acadians accepted the invitation of the Saint-Domingue government, surreptitiously left their scene of their exile, and ultimately found themselves impressed into forced work gangs at the French naval base of Môle St. Nicolas on Saint-Domingue's northern coastline. In 1767, an additional 240 Acadians, led by their erstwhile parish priest, pooled their resources, chartered the *Pitt*, a merchantman, and probably sailed for the St. John River Valley in New Brunswick or Quebec. Only a handful of Acadians appear to have remained permanently in Connecticut.[47]

Massachusetts

The Acadian experience in Massachusetts has traditionally been viewed as the darkest chapter of the diaspora. The conditions encountered by the exiles in Massachusetts, however, were generally no worse than those which they endured in other Atlantic seaboard colonies.

Because of Governor Shirley's role in the conspiracy to deport Nova Scotia's Acadian population, the Bay Colony received at least twice the number of exiles transported to any other British North American colony—perhaps as many as 1,500. The first Acadians arrived at Boston on November 12, 1755, and, within one week, there were approximately 2,000 Acadians aboard British ships in Massachusetts Bay. Most of these early Acadians, however, were destined for other seaboard colonies and remained in Massachusetts waters only long enough for their ships to be refitted. The *Seaflower*, which cast anchor at Boston on November 19, 1755, carried the colony's first permanent Acadian residents, 206 former Pisiquid settlers. They were followed on December 13 by 136 Minas Basin Acadians aboard the *Swallow*, and on December 26 by a large, but undetermined number of exiles. Between December 26 and January 15, four more shiploads of Acadians were cast upon Massachusetts' shores. The final contingent of Acadian immigrants, ninety French Neutrals who were stubbornly attempting to return to Nova Scotia from exile in Georgia were arrested and detained when they landed south of Boston in August 1756.[48]

Like Acadians elsewhere, these exiles contracted smallpox upon contact with the established Anglo-American population, and, having no natural immunity to this disease, their numbers were decimated by it. Yet, because of the virulent francophobia among the native Bostonians no governmental assistance was immediately forthcoming, and only a single Anglo—future Massachusetts governor Thomas Hutchinson—appears to have stepped forward to provide the exiles with a modicum of relief.[49]

Indeed, the Massachusetts government—like its counterparts throughout the British North American empire—was far more concerned with distributing and controlling the

Acadians than with their general welfare. Upon arrival, each group of exiles was distributed among the "Country towns," which were expected to provide housing and presumably food for the exiles, but only during their initial winter in the colony. The Acadians thereafter were expected to be self-supporting, and local justices of the peace and overseers of the poor were empowered by the colonial legislature "to employ, bind out or support said Inhabitants of Nova Scotia" should they display any abhorrence for work.[50]

Eventually realizing that the Acadians were overwhelmingly farmers lacking the skills required by the provincial job market, the provincial assembly, on March 1, 1756, required those local Massachusetts officials charged with oversight of the exiled population to provide "implements of husbandry, and those for weaving, spinning, and other handicraft work according to the capacity of the individual." Those failing to take advantage of this generous offer faced immediate disciplinary action by the welfare agents. By early April, for example, sufficient Acadian children had been forcibly indentured to elicit an outcry from Acadian leaders in at least six Massachusetts communities. This outburst caused the provincial legislature to moderate its "workfare" policy, and local welfare agents were prohibited from dividing Acadian families except in cases of dire need. The government also periodically investigated reports of malfeasance, or nonfeasance on the part of local welfare officials and routinely interceded in cases where complaints were justified.[51]

The provincial government, on the other hand, disregarded Acadian protests regarding governmental efforts to control their movements. The first Acadian exiles sent to the "Country towns" apparently enjoyed virtual freedom of movement, and many reputedly escaped to the St. John River Valley, from which they apparently made their way to Quebec. Many Acadian men also appear to have found employment as sailors aboard merchant vessels and fishing boats sailing from Massachusetts ports. Finally, many other exiles appear to have wandered from town to town for months in search of friends and relatives. Such freedom of movement by potential fifth columnists greatly disturbed the native population. On April 15, 1756, the provincial legislature responded with legislation prohibiting ship captains from hiring Acadians, and, in May 1757, a second act prohibited the exiles from leaving the corporate limits of the towns to which they had been assigned under pain of a fine for the first offense, flogging for the second.[52]

The regimentation of the Acadian population by the provincial government was greatly relaxed with the end of the Seven Years' War in 1763. Acadians, in large numbers, abandoned the towns to which they had been assigned in 1755-1756 and began to congregate on the colony's larger urban areas. With communications between the various Acadian groups thus reestablished, the exiles in Massachusetts, like those in other Atlantic seaboard colonies, petitioned the French government for resettlement in France, and, when French assistance failed to materialize, at least 300 Massachusetts Acadians left the colony for French Saint-Domingue. An additional 300 attempted to follow their countrymen shortly thereafter but were prevented from doing so by the provincial government. Meanwhile, several hundred other Massachusetts Acadians secretly left the colony for Quebec by way of Lake Champlain. Another party of Acadians, numbering 116 persons, sailed from Boston for St. Pierre and Miquelon, barren, wind-swept islands near Newfoundland which were France's sole remaining North American possessions, arriving at Miquelon on October 1, 1763.[53]

The Acadians remaining in Massachusetts then demanded work and improved living conditions or British-subsidized resettlement in Canada. The former demand was rejected, but, having grown weary of the Acadians, the provincial assembly entertained the second request. Acadian delegates were dispatched to Canada to confer with the Canadian governor, who agreed to permit the Massachusetts Acadians to resettle in Canada, provided they took an oath of allegiance to Britain. On June 2, 1766, 720 Acadians in Boston, 140 in Salem, and significant numbers of Acadians in other Massachusetts towns took an unconditional oath of allegiance to King George and prepared to leave the Bay Colony.

Few Acadians possessed the resources to leave Massachusetts by ship, and these generally sailed to Quebec.

The remainder then walked overland, through the wilderness to either their Nova Scotian homeland, or to Quebec. Those who reached Nova Scotia after a four-month trek through present-day Maine and New Brunswick found their homeland occupied by former New Englanders. In fact, "as early as 1763, 12,000 new [*i.e.*, English] inhabitants had settled in what had formerly been Acadia."[54] Many Acadians were apparently unable to reconcile themselves to the new state of things, and many chose to settle in the Petit Codiac River Valley of New Brunswick, which, unlike the pre-dispersal Acadian settlements, had not been occupied by transplanted New Englanders.

Post-Dispersal Nova Scotia

Other, more determined, exiles from New England chose to accept the lands—usually forty acres per family[55]—in the northern and western extremities of Nova Scotia which the provincial government offered them, lands the British considered undesirable. According to Muriel K. Roy, the first Acadian settlements established in Nova Scotia after 1763 were Chezzetcook and Prospect, near Halifax. These settlements were founded by Acadians who had been held in Halifax detention centers during the Seven Years' War. Additional returning exiles chose to settle along the Strait of Canso, the coast of which, before the diaspora, had been the locus of much fishing activity. Other Acadians found a home along the western Nova Scotian coastline. By 1767, there were Acadian settlements at the mouth of Baie Ste-Marie, near present-day Church Point (Pointe-de-l'Eglise), and at Tousquet and Pobomcoup. Refugees from St. Pierre and Miquelon established the first post-dispersal Acadian settlements on Cape Breton Island in 1767. Settling in the Chéticamp[56] and Margaree areas, they were joined, in the 1780s, by Acadians from Prince Edward Island.[57]

Prince Edward Island[58]

The Acadians who returned to the Canadian Maritimes from exile in Massachusetts during the mid-1760s were not the only Acadians in the region. It is indeed a popular misconception that all of the Acadians were deported from the region in 1755. Only 6,000-7,000 of Nova Scotia's 12,000-18,000 resident Acadians were removed from their homeland during the Grand Dérangement. Those who escaped deportation became fugitives. Hundreds made their way to Prince Edward Island (then called Ile St-Jean), a French possession which had been established earlier in the eighteenth century by Acadians no longer wishing to remain under British rule; by 1758, there were between 3,400 and 5,000 Acadians residing there.[59] Following the fall of Louisbourg on neighboring Cape Breton Island in 1758, Prince Edward Island was occupied by British forces who deported to France two-thirds of the Acadian population. Upon arrival in France, most of these deportees lived in slums in France's Atlantic port cities. Most of the remaining P.E.I. Acadians made their way either to Quebec, while a much smaller group migrated to St. Pierre and Miquelon islands. A few Acadians, unwilling to run from the English any longer, hid in the woods on Prince Edward Island for the duration of the Seven Years' War. In 1763, British authorities discovered the existence of approximately thirty families, "miserably poor, who had taken refuge in the thick of the woods." These families constituted the bulk of the early postbellum Acadian community on Prince Edward Island. According to the 1768 census of the region, the island's 203 Acadian inhabitants[60] resided at St. Pierre, Tracadie, Rustico, and Malpèque, villages in which the exiles worked as fishermen for British entrepreneurs.[61]

The status of these fishermen changed drastically in 1769. In that year the island was established as a British province, and, with the establishment of British rule, the Acadian landholders were deprived of their land titles and reduced to tenantry as ownership of their lands was acquired by Englishmen.[62] Having endured the rigors of life in the wilderness during the post expulsion, many Acadians on Prince Edward Island balked at this latest British outrage and opted to emigrate.[63]

New Brunswick and Madawaska

The fate of the Prince Edward Island Acadians was shared
by their confrères in neighboring New Brunswick. Prior to the
Grand Dérangement, New Brunswick boasted only a few,
widely scattered Acadian settlements. The oldest one, along the
St. John River, contained only a "handful" of settlers, who,
lacking many basic land-clearing implements, found life quite
difficult.[64] Other Acadian settlements were found near present-
day Memramcook, at Petit Codiac, and at Miramichi, along the
northern New Brunswick coast.

The size of these tiny settlements grew dramatically in 1755,
as thousands of Acadian refugees sought refuge from the British
deportation campaign. Some of the first refugees reached the
lower St. John River in late 1755, after members of thirty-two
Acadian families placed aboard an English snow[65] rose up, and
after intense hand-to-hand fighting, took control of the vessel
that was destined to carry them into exile in South Carolina.
Charles Belliveau, one of the former captives and an
experienced seaman, piloted the ship to the St. John River, along
which they attempted to settle. This settlement, however, was
soon harassed by English Rangers, and the refugees were forced
to migrate inland, where they encountered a French military
force commanded by Charles des Champs de Boishébert. They
were subsequently joined by other Acadians fleeing the
deportation attempt in the Beaubassin/Fort Beauséjour area.
According to historian William O. Raymond, approximately
1,000 Acadians had congregated along the St. John River by
early 1756. Lacking the resources to assist them, Boishébert sent
many of the exiles to Quebec. Many others, however, remained
in the vicinity of present-day Frederickton, cleared several
hundred acres of land, and attempted to start life anew.[66]

The exiles' resettlement efforts were interrupted by a British
invasion in September 1758. Intimidated by the size of Colonel
Robert Monckton's 2,000-man army, Boishébert's much smaller
force withdrew to Quebec, leaving the hapless Acadians to fend
for themselves. In late October, Monckton's soldiers surprised
one Acadian settlement and took 100 prisoners, who were
subsequently sent to Halifax "to be transmitted from thence to

Europe."[67]   Other St. John Acadians evaded a second British attempt to capture prisoners in November, 1756, but many of these fugitives were forced to migrate to Quebec when the British troops destroyed their homes and crops.[68]

Only the most stubborn and determined Acadians remained along the St. John River, reoccupying their devastated farmsteads.   On the night of January 28 or 29, 1759, a band of British Rangers attacked Sainte-Anne, the largest remaining Acadian settlement along the St. John River, and set ablaze all of the homes there.   More than twenty-five prisoners were taken, and those prisoners who refused to assist the attackers in burning Acadian homes were put to death, including women and children.   The survivors either "went up to Canada or sought refuge in the woods."[69]

The 1759 refugees from the St. John Valley hoped to find asylum in Quebec, but the city was soon besieged by British forces.   After the French citadel's fall, many of the fugitives decided to return to their adopted home and reach an accommodation with the local British authorities.   On October 18, 1759, two Acadians representing 200 of their now demoralized countrymen visited British military installations along the lower St. John River and requested permission to remain on their lands if they took an unconditional oath of allegiance to Britain.   Charles Lawrence, the governor of Nova Scotia to whom this request was referred, refused and sent ships "for having them immediately transported to Halifax as prisoners of war, until they can be sent to England." The 200 Acadians deported during this operation arrived at Halifax on February 11, 1760.[70]

Despite the constant threat of military harassment and deportation, a small number of Acadians remained in the St. John River Valley.   In 1767, the Acadian presence along the St. John was formally authorized, after the exiles had taken an unconditional oath of allegiance to Britain.   The St. John Acadians affirmed their loyalty to Britain through dedicated service during the American Revolution, yet, upon the conclusion of the war of independence and the onset of Loyalist immigration into present-day New Brunswick, local British authorities permitted the Loyalists to expropriate, usually through force or violence, the lands of the Acadians, who the newcomers called "French Squatters."   When the evicted Acadians protested their treatment to higher authorities, they were told that they must relocate and settle the less desirable lands along the upper St. John River, in the Madawaska region, where a small Acadian settlement[71] had existed since 1768. The British government promised that they would be given titles to these new properties after three years of uninterrupted settlement.[72]

The vanguard of the Acadian migration from the lower St. John Valley to Madawaska began in June 1785. Their first farmsteads were in the vicinity of present-day Beaulieu, Maine. Other immigrants followed the next year and settled in the Verte River Valley nearby, and small-scale immigration would continue for some time. But not all immigrants remained. Despite British assurances that land titles would be forthcoming after three years, many settlers had to wait at least five years before titles were issued. Unwilling to endure further their ill-treatment by the British, many Acadians abandoned their developing farms and moved on.[73]

The trials of the Acadians on New Brunswick's upper coast paralleled those of their cousins in the St. John Valley far to the south. Under the leadership of Abbé Le Guerne, most of the refugees along the upper coast (some estimates place the figure at approximately 4,000) made their way to the Miramichi area. Having fled their homes with little more than the clothes they carried on their backs, these refugees, many of whom were women whose husbands had already been sent into exile from Beaubassin, lacked adequate shelter, food and clothing. Pierre de Rigaud, the marquis de Vaudreuil, governor of Canada, described their plight:

> Acadian mothers see their babes die at the breast not having wherewith to nourish them. The majority of the people cannot appear abroad for want of clothes to cover their nakedness. Many have died. The number of the sick is considerable, and those convalescent cannot regain their strength on account of the wretched quality of their food, being often under the necessity of eating horse meat extremely lean, sea-cow, and skins of oxen. Such of the state of the Acadians.[74]

Starvation, exposure, and disease claimed hundreds of Miramichi Acadians during their first winter in exile. The dire prospects faced by the Miramichi colony caused several hundred survivors to migrate to Quebec the following spring. There, they remained until the fall of New France's capital in 1759. Many hundreds, nevertheless, remained and attempted to start life anew. This task, made difficult by the sterile soil of the settlement region and the debilitated condition of the survivors, became virtually impossible in 1758 when British search and destroy missions designed to protect British communication lines during the anticipated Quebec campaign prevented the refugees from either farming or fishing in coastal waters. Starvation again set in and the Miramichi Acadians faced the prospect of another "winter of discontent."[75]

The problems of the Miramichi Acadians were shared by those Acadians established in the Petit Codiac River Valley near the Nova Scotian border. Unlike the Miramichi refugees, however, most of these Acadians had settled in present-day New Brunswick before 1755, and they thus were not disarmed by British forces shortly before the onset of the *Grand Dérangement*. Led by Joseph Broussard *dit* Beausoleil, the Petit Codiac Acadians formed para-military resistance units that conducted raids deep into Nova Scotia and even operated a privateer against British vessels on the Bay of Fundy.[76]

Like many of their counterparts along the northern New Brunswick coast, the Petit Codiac Acadians were disheartened by the fall of Louisbourg, the French bastion in the region, in 1758. Faced with the prospect of famine and no longer sustained by the hope of a French military victory over their oppressors, these Acadians were compelled to surrender in late 1758 and early 1759. They were sent to detention centers in Halifax, where, with the exception of work-release programs allowing them to maintain the Bay of Fundy dykes for the English families who had occupied their farms, they remained for the duration of the war. In 1764, many of the Halifax detainees contemplated reestablishment in Saint-Domingue, but eventually sailed for the Mississippi Valley in November 1764. Two hundred and thirty-one of them arrived unannounced at New Orleans in February 1765. Others went to St. Pierre and

Miquelon.[77]

Not all of the northern New Brunswick Acadians surrendered to British authorities. Others stubbornly remained on their new farmsteads at Memramcook, at Cocagne, at the mouth of the Miramichi River, at Restigouche, at Caraquet,[78] and at Nepisiguit (present-day Bathurst), taking refuge "in the Baie des Chaleurs area. Some of these settlements remained quite large throughout the early post-dispersal era. In 1760, for example, Restigouche harbored approximately 1,000 Acadian refugees. The persistence of these settlements drew the unwelcome attention of the British military. In October 1761, for example, a force of British Highlanders led by Captain Roderick MacKenzie raided numerous Acadian coastal settlements and succeeded in taking 787 prisoners. Of these, 335 were taken to Halifax, while the remainder were permitted to remain because of illness or advanced age and because of the limited space aboard MacKenzie's vessels. Following such raids, the surviving Acadians routinely withdrew temporarily to the Baie des Chaleurs area, Gaspé and Quebec, only to return whenever the prospects for permanent settlement seemed more favorable.[79]

Sufficient Acadians thus remained to maintain the viability of these settlements until the presence of the Acadian refugees in this area was formally sanctioned by the British government in 1764. The early postdispersal settlements provided the foundation for the reconstruction of Acadian society in northern New Brunswick. By 1803, eighty-eight percent of the 3,729 Acadians in New Brunswick resided either in the early post-dispersal settlements or in communities adjacent to them.[80]

England and France

The travails of the Acadians who eluded capture along the northern New Brunswick coast were exceeded by those less fortunate refugees who fell into the hands of British raiders in the late 1750s and early 1760s. These prisoners routinely faced imprisonment in Halifax or deportation to Europe. For example, most of the Acadians who had fled to Ile St. Jean were taken prisoner by English forces in 1758 and over 3,000 of them were deported to France aboard cartel ships. There, they congregated in the slums of the northeastern coastal cities. France's initial Acadian refugees were subsequently joined by several hundred additional exiles taken as prisoners of war by British forces at the fall of Quebec City in 1759. Like their predecessors, they lived in poverty in the ports of St. Malo and Morlaix. Their numbers were augmented in 1763 by 753 Acadians from England, survivors of the 1,500 Acadians rejected by Virginia and sent across the Atlantic to Great Britain in 1755.[81]

Though a minority of the Acadians in France, the Acadians from England were particularly significant, for they played a crucial role in shaping the outcome of the French effort to "repatriate" the exiles. The so-called repatriation of the Acadian exiles to France resulted from the sympathy felt by French diplomats attempting to negotiate an end to the Seven Years War in England for the misery and deprivation experienced by those Acadians in English coastal detention centers. Living in virtual imprisonment, under conditions far worse than any experienced by their relatives in the eastern seaboard colonies, these Acadians had watched helplessly as half their fellow exiles died from epidemic diseases, particularly smallpox. Moved with pity for what he saw, M. de la Rochette, secretary to the French minister plenipotentiary, circulated a letter among the Acadians in England in which he urged the exiles to cooperate with French diplomatic efforts to liberate them, stating "your treatment in France will be still more advantageous than you expect." These circular letters helped secure the cooperation of the skeptical Acadians, who, in turn, apprised their relatives in the eastern seaboard colonies of the forthcoming diplomatic negotiations on their behalf; which, in turn, prompted the Acadians in the British North American colonies to petition the French king for repatriation.[82]

Only those Acadians in England, however, were "repatriated" to France. Before crossing the English Channel, these Acadians expected special treatment, particularly resettlement upon fertile land and the reestablishment of their pre-dispersal lifestyle; these dreams were shattered immediately upon arrival in France. Like the Acadians who had preceded them to the mother country, they found themselves literally dumped in coastal cities, where, except for a small welfare subsidy (insufficient to pay either rent or food), they were abandoned by the crown. Indeed, after being temporarily housed in makeshift reception centers (sometimes abandoned military barracks),[83] many Acadians found themselves literally forced to live in the streets, with no prospect of improving their lot. The economies of the French coastal cities were devastated by the war and British blockade and thus offered few job opportunities; the Acadians, on the other hand, generally lacked the job skills demanded by urban job markets and thus could not find employment where jobs existed. Fully cognizant of the Acadians' plight, many unscrupulous French businessmen and landowners attempted to exploit the exiles ruthlessly. One landowner suggested that the government institute "workfare" and send the Acadians to work in his mines, while other "land sharks and swindlers" attempted to have the Acadians reduced to the status of peasants and employed as workers on French estates. Such was the unscrupulousness of these individuals that the French minister of state, Etienne François, duc de Choiseul-Stainville, an individual not generally known for his compassion, was compelled to intervene on the Acadians behalf. In 1765, he established a small group of exiles on Belle-Ile-en-Mer, a rocky, wind-swept island off the Breton coast. The colony endured seven years and collapsed, the result of crop failure, drought, livestock epidemics, and the opposition of native Frenchmen.[84]

Other colonization attempts within France met with the same fate. In 1772, acting upon royal instructions, French Minister of State Jean Berton placed 1,500 Acadians on a 15,000-arpent Poitou estate owned by the marquis Perusse des Cars. Under the terms of the estate's occupation, the Acadians were to function as sharecroppers who would develop and farm the long-neglected Perusse manor. The colony began inauspiciously, for housing was unavailable on the estate and the Acadians were forced to rent rooms at exorbitant prices in nearby villages. In addition, the sterile soil on the estate lacked sufficient nutrients for the crops to mature. In late 1775, the members of the Acadian colony, which had come to be called the Grand Ligne settlement,

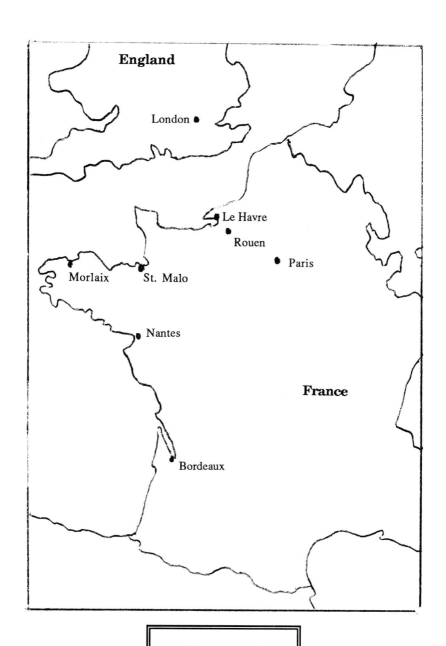

France and England, ca. 1768

voted to abandon the Perusse estate and, by mid-1776, only 160 Acadians remained on the property.[85]

With the failure of the Grand Ligne experiment, French officials again sought out potential settlement sites within the realm. In 1777, for example, French Minister of Finance Jacques Necker proposed the settlement of the French Acadians at Corsica. This proposal was duly rejected by a meeting of Acadian representatives.[86]

With the failure of the Corsica proposal, the Acadians in France sought to find their own solution to their dilemma. In mid-October 1777, twenty-two Acadians secured permission to migrate to Louisiana from the Spanish ambassador to France. An undetermined number of other exiles from Nantes and St. Malo secretly travelled to Prince Edward Island, Halifax, and other Nova Scotian ports via the English Island of Guernsey.[87]

Many of the Acadians remaining in France grew increasingly disillusioned with government-sponsored colonization attempts, and they strenuously resisted the efforts, in 1783 and 1784, of French soldier of fortune Henri Peyroux de la Coudrenière and Acadian cobbler Olivier Terrio (Theriot) to organize a massive migration to Louisiana. Although anxious to resolve the festering Acadian problem, the French government refused to help subsidize the migration because Louisiana had become a Spanish colony following the Treaty of Paris (1763). The Spanish government, on the other hand, was anxious to recruit French Acadians to bolster the small population of its sprawling, and militarily vulnerable, Louisiana colony. An accord was finally reached between the French and Spanish governments in late 1784, and over 1,500 Acadians (roughly seventy percent of all Acadians remaining in France), whose initial scepticism about the venture was overcome by the involvement of the Spanish goverment, volunteered for the colonizaton expedition. Between mid-May and mid-October 1785, 1,596 Acadians turned their backs on France and sailed to New Orleans aboard seven transport vessels.[88]

Saint-Domingue

Choiseul's attempt to establish an Acadian colony at Belle-Ile-en-Mer may well have stemmed from his own pangs of conscience, for he himself had earlier exploited the exiles' misfortune. At the end of the Seven Years' War in 1763, Choiseul desperately attempted to rebuild France's shattered overseas empire. France's few remaining overseas possessions required reinforcement, but few native Frenchmen were willing to leave their homeland for an uncertain future in the tropics. Choiseul therefore turned to the Acadians as a potential pool of colonists, and the exiles were not entirely unreceptive to his overtures.[89]

Particularly susceptible to Choiseul's recruitment campaign were the Acadians remaining in exile in the English seaboard colonies. In 1763, M. de la Rochette's circular letter to the Acadians detained in England had been smuggled by the exiles to Acadian communities throughout North America. Heartened by the French effort to liberate them, numerous Acadian groups petitioned Louis XV for "repatriation." The French monarch, influenced by Choiseul's grand strategic designs, consequently ordered the governors of Saint-Domingue and Martinique to dispatch ships to the seaboard colonies "to rescue the prisoners, particularly those of Boston and New York."[90]

Before initiating the proposed rescue operation, Choiseul, fearing the potential opposition of officials in the seaboard colonies, attempted to guage the British response to this venture through diplomatic channels. In late fall, Choiseul instructed M. de Guerchy, the newly appointed French ambassador to England, to discuss a potential Acadian withdrawal from British North America. Guerchy responded on December 6, 1763, stating that, the provisions of the Treaty of Paris (1763) notwithstanding, the British government would, under no circumstances, allow the Acadians to leave. The French were consequently forced to devise a policy of removing the exiles surreptitiously. Beginning in late 1763 and continuing throughout early 1764, French merchantmen sailing from the French Antilles to the ports of Maryland, Pennsylvania, New

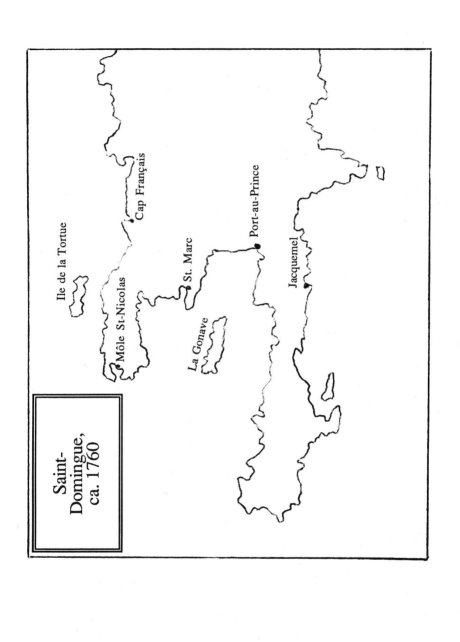

Saint-
Domingue,
ca. 1760

Ile de la Tortue

Cap Français

Môle St-Nicolas

St. Marc

La Gonave

Port-au-Prince

Jacquemel

York, and Massachusetts routinely took on a few Acadian passengers for the return voyage. This practice assumed the mantle of official policy on September 19, 1764, when Versailles ordered French merchantmen engaged in the American/Antillian trade to exchange their cargoes of rum and molasses for Acadian passengers and lumber which could be used to construct dwellings for the transplanted exiles.[91]

To encourage Acadian participation in this operation, the French government secretly employed a recruiting agent in New York. This agent, a prominent merchant "by the name of Hanson,"[92] a man with influential friends in Cap Français,[93] was directed to circulate the June 26, 1764, proclamation by Charles-Henri, comte d'Estaing,[94] who had become governor of Saint-Domingue the previous April, promising "the Acadians land and sustenance until they became self-sufficient." The French government also promised to absorb the cost of the voyage.[95]

Such assurances were necessary, d'Estaing believed, to secure a sufficient number of workers to begin the massive Môle Saint-Nicolas naval base project which had been ordered by Versailles in 1763. An essential part of Choiseul's plan to strengthen the island's defenses, the construction of a major naval base in northern Saint-Domingue was intended to permit France to control the vital Caribbean sea lanes in wartime.[96] This project was begun in February 1764, but it immediately became apparent that the demands of constructing such a large military facility would severely tax the resources of the colonial administration, even one as generously supported as that of Saint-Domingue. The prospective naval base site was situated in the midst of a dense jungle. Just clearing the site would be a long, back-breaking task requiring a large work force, and Choiseul and d'Estaing both saw in the Acadians a potential labor pool. Through Choiseul's efforts, local intendants, in 1763-1764, reportedly recruited for resettlement in the Antilles approximately 2,000 Acadians who had been either exiled to France from Louisbourg (1758) or who had been "repatriated" to France from England (1763).[97] Few, if any, of these Acadians, however, appear to have been sent to Saint-Domingue. The Acadians from France were reinforced by hundreds of

Acadians recruited in the Eastern seaboard colonies. And this exodus from the British colonies would undoubtedly have been significantly larger had Hanson not extracted exorbitant rates from individual passengers for transportation to the French Antilles in addition to the 150-*livre* per passenger subsidy paid to him by the Saint-Domingue government. (The mutually agreed upon subsidy was intended to cover all transportation costs.)

Despite Hanson's dishonesty, which nearly subverted the Acadian relocation scheme, sufficient numbers of exiles reached Saint-Domingue to permit the Môle Saint-Nicolas project to begin. Between September 23, 1764, and January 26, 1765, Hanson's ships transported 418 Acadians to Môle Saint-Nicolas alone.[98] Drawn from Hanson's hapless victims, the first contingent of Acadian workers—consisting of approximately 400 individuals, all apparently from New England[99]—was sent to Môle Saint-Nicolas, where they arrived around February 2, 1764. In conformity with a plan devised and implemented by the chevalier de Montreuil, d'Estaing's predecessor, in confirmity with broad instructions from Choiseul, the Acadians were to be promised 10 *carreaux*[100] of land in exchange for clearing the base site and for serving as laborers in various stages of the construction. The Acadians, who were to be given clothing, food, and tents, were to be established near a source of fresh water. The exiles, who would receive no salary, were to be "employed on the *corvée.*"[101] If necessary, slaves were to be hired and given the same support extended to the Acadians.[102]

The Acadians grudgingly endured their new status as forced laborers only because of the promised land grants which would allow them to reestablish their agrarian way of life. Ill-will between the Acadians and their French administrators, however, became increasingly evident as the project progressed, largely as a result of the officials' arrogance[103] and the conditions the exiles were forced to endure: The settlement's source of drinking water was of dubious salubrity, and, within a week of their arrival, the exiles were stricken with severe diarrhea, perhaps the beginnings of amoebic dysentery; by mid-February, many of the Acadians were showing signs of scurvy as a result of their inadequate diet. Health concerns were exacerbated by the occasional reduction of food rations to Acadian children. By mid-March, the Acadians had filed a formal protest, yet, by mid-summer, Acadian children were dying of scurvy, while the local administrator, one Saltoris, "daily us[ed] milk in his coffee." But even these concerns were overshadowed by the discovery by the Acadians, during a mid-February land survey, that their prospective farm sites were unacceptable. The Acadians immediately petitioned the government for small land grants on more fertile plots.[104] The local administrator suggested that the governor accept their request but suggested that the Acadian land grants be reduced to only two *carreaux.* [105]

The problems of the Môle Saint-Nicolas settlement were compounded by the periodic arrival of large numbers of Acadians, all of whom also expected land grants. By the beginning of June numerous Acadians had fallen victim to scurvy, malaria, and other tropical diseases. Lacking physicians and a hospital, those Acadians contracting disease had little hope of recovery. Seven Acadians are reported to have died in May and the death toll climbed throughout the summer.[106]

The Môle administrators failed to report these critical problems to their superiors. Thus d'Estaing learned of the situation and begin to take corrective measures only during an inspection tour on July 7. A new administrator was appointed, but he proved to be no more capable or honest than his predecessor.[107] Meanwhile the problems facing the Acadians grew increasingly severe as new waves of immigrants began to arrive periodically in late 1764 and early 1765. Of the 938 Acadians sent to Môle Saint-Nicolas in 1764, only 672 remained at the beginning of 1765.[108]

Despite such frightful mortality, the colonial government continued to send Acadians to Môle. One hundred and eighty-eight exiles, apparently transported from New England by Hanson, debarked at Môle during the first four months of 1765. These Acadians were joined by hundreds of Germans who had originally been recruited for the French colonization project in Guiana. (See below, *Guiana.*) By mid-1765, the German influx had caused the Môle settlement to triple in size.[109]

The resulting strain on the settlement's meagre resources

caused a precipitous decline in the already poor quality of life in
the Môle area. Local adminsitrators reported in 1765 that their
Acadian workers had grown quite apathetic and discouraged.
The situation gradually became so severe that, on September 21,
1765, d'Estaing was compelled to notifiy Choiseul that

> the complaints of the colonists of Santo Domingo . . . have begun
> to surface. I was there [Môle] and I found some men bewildered,
> without shelter, dying under bushes, abundantly furnished
> with hardtack and saltmeat which they cannot eat, as well as
> tools which are of inferior quality. They curse an existence so
> filled with discouragement that they despair. . . . The worst
> criminal would prefer the galleys and the torture associated
> with that punishment rather than stay in this horrible place. No
> one would believe such a place exists. . . . Only constraint keeps
> the residents there.[110]

The result of these conditions was an inevitable exodus from the
district.   Beginning in August 1765, numerous Acadians
petitioned d'Estaing for permission to leave Môle. Few were
granted permission to leave, prompting some Acadians to
desert, with some of the first deserters migrating to the adjacent
district of Jean Rabel. Desertion would continue in significant
numbers for at least two years. These deserters, it seems, found
life at least as difficult in other areas of Saint-Domingue.[111]
     Profiting from the deserters' experience, a majority of the
Môle Acadians chose to remain in the district.   Desertion
offered the life of a fugitive, and, even if they were granted
asylum in another district, they would have to carve themselves
a niche with essentially no resources. Most of the Acadians at
Môle, on the other hand, had built homes, started gardens, and,
in some cases, begun to acquire livestock. Many Acadians also
found at least occasional employment as carpenters, masons,
and laborers for the continuing construction of the naval base.
Such income proved increasingly important after the summer of
1766, when the government ceased to provide rations to the
Acadians. It is thus hardly surprising that the district's records
indicate that, by the mid-1770s, the overwhelming majority of
Acadians at Môle were artisans.[112]
     The Môle colony was the largest, though not the only,

significant Acadian settlement at Saint-Domingue. In August 1764, 180 Acadians arriving at Port-au-Prince from New England, apparently aboard Hanson's ships, were sent by the colonial administration to Mirebalais, a recently established settlement in the hill country, about thirty miles to the northeast, where, it was hoped, the immigrants would establish truck farms and small coffee plantations.[113] These Acadians were furnished temporary housing in Mirebalais and at the plantations in the area until permanent housing was available. Because of the opposition by local planters to the distribution of land to the exiles as well as an unidentified epidemic, forcing the immigrants to work as laborers on existing coffee plantations, the Mirebalais Acadian community appears to have dispersed rapidly, with many exiles migrating to other areas where land ownership was possible. Some of these Acadians made their home, at least temporarily, at Boucan Carré, at the Capuchin canton, and, in larger numbers, at Montagne Terrible. Even here, however, the Acadians, lacking the capital to start their own coffee plantations, were forced to seek employment as laborers and managers on established plantations.[114]

The growth of the Acadian communities at Mirebalais and Môle Saint-Nicolas is very difficult to determine, in part because of the destruction of many records during the Haitian Revolution and in part from the scarcity of printed works on the subject. Numerous published sources, based entirely on speculation, had suggested that many of the Saint-Domingue Acadians left the colony for Louisiana in the mid-to-late 1760s.[115] The documentary record in Louisiana, however, makes it quite clear that few, if any, Saint-Domingue Acadians migrated to the Mississippi Valley. It is also highly unlikely that the Môle Saint-Nicolas and Mirebalais Acadians left for France or other French possessions. What is apparent is that, the Acadians, after sustaining frightening losses to tropical diseases, malnutrition, and scurvy, gradually adapted to their new and radically different surroundings. Compounding the problem of adaptation were the island's social structure, which effectively lacked a niche for yeoman farmers, the difficulty of securing sufficient land to launch a viable farming operation, and the necessity of adapting their farming practices to tropical crops. Unable to surmount these difficulties, many Acadians chose the path of least resistance and sought to integrate themselves into the island's socio-economic system as plantation laborers, plantation artisans, plantation overseers/managers, and, far more rarely, plantation owners. Over the years many of these Acadians intermarried with other French colonists of their economic caste thus solidifying their growing ties to the island and its plantation system.

Their affiliation with the plantation system forced them to flee the Haitian Revolution of the 1790s. Like the other Saint-Domingue refugees, some of them made their way to ports on the Eastern seabord. Others undoubtedly migrated, with the largest single group of refugees, first to Santiago de Cuba, and, in 1809, from Santiago de Cuba to New Orleans.[116]

Martinique

As with Saint-Domingue, much is known about the arrival of the island's first Acadian immigrants, but little is known of their subsequent fate.[117] On April 20, 1756, a Martinique official notified Versailles that a New York-bound British ship carrying approximately 300 Acadian deportees from the Port Royal area had been blown off course by winter storms, which had driven the vessel to Antigua, a British possession in the Leeward Islands. Antiguan authorities sent the exiles to St. Kitts, where they remained from January 25, 1756, to April 1, 1756.[118]

Unable or unwilling to support the Acadians any longer, the St. Kitts government transported some of the exiles to, and summarily abandoned them at, the Dutch colony of St. Eustatius (called St. Eustache by the French). Forced by the colonial government to support these unwelcome interlopers, the British consul at St. Eustatius provided the Acadians with food, but in such small quantities that the exiles were forced to turn to private charity to survive. Governor Jan de Windt, Jr., evidently afraid that the Acadians would become a permanent burden on the island's population, urgently sought relief from the French government of Martinique. [119]

Windt's appeal for aid was apparently honored by the Martinique government, for twenty-eight Acadian exiles subsequently made their way to that French island. Upon arrival at Martinique, the exiles requested passage to either Cape Breton Island or Quebec, and their accommodating hosts replied that they would "avail [themselves] of the first opportunity to send them there." The documentary record, however, suggests that, the officials' assurances notwithstanding, these exiles were forced to remain in the Antilles.[120]

French Guiana

On December 26, 1762, Choiseul directed France's regional administrative chiefs—the intendants—to recruit colonists, including the Acadian exiles residing in their respective districts, for French Guiana and the Antilles. This recruitment effort was later broadened to include the Acadian refugee camps on St. Pierre and Miquelon islands. The intendants were moderately successful in finding colonists for France's prosperous possessions in the Antilles, particularly Saint-Domingue, but Guiana, a backwater region whose insalubrious climate was notorious in France and its dependencies, initially proved unappealing to the exiles. The written response of the Miquelon Acadians to pressure from French colonial administrators vividly reflects the exiles' well-grounded fears about the much ballyhooed "haven where we can be happy":

> Everything [about Guiana] seems advantageous to us indeed ... but, we beseech you to note that [resettlement in] a country as hot as Cayenne[121] would cost us too dearly—as much as [resettlement in] the hot countries [*i.e.,* the southern English seaboard colonies], where the English transported our people, has cost us—because the climate [is] so excessively hot in comparison to the temperate and much more healthy North American climate of our homeland. No matter what the proposed advantages [of emigrating to Cayenne] are, and no matter what threats are leveled against us for taking this course of action, we value life above everything else, and we shall never agree to leave the climate here.[122]

Because of the Acadians' stiff initial resistance to the Guiana colonization proposal, the French government sent "hucksters" instructed to sing the praises of Guiana to Switzerland, Italy, Bavaria and Alsace.[123] Depicting the jungle backwater as a "promised land" where two crops a year were possible, these colonization promoters assured each potential colonist that he would receive, in addition to a land grant, assistance from the French government in the form of money— a subsidy of fifty *livres* per family and an additional ten *livres* per child—plus free food, housing, and clothing for two years. These grassroots promotions were soon supplemented by official French recruiting agents in Germany and in Alsace.[124]

The response of the unsuspecting, land-hungry peasants was enthusiastic, particularly in the Palatinate. Indeed, German recruitment far exceeded Choiseul's most optimistic expectations. By late July 1763, 8,000 German recruits had reportedly congregated at the Atlantic ports of Rochefort and Saint-Jean d'Angély awaiting transportation to South America.

The remarkable success of German recruitment effort allowed Choiseul to formulate a much grander vision of Guiana colonization. Disregarding advice from colonial experts to limit the size of the proposed influx in order to avoid overtaxing the colony's meagre resources, Choiseul decided to send to Guiana as many colonists as possible, as quickly as possible. The first wave of colonists—numbering 1,780 persons[125]—began leaving France in May 1763, and large scale emigration to Guiana continued throughout 1764, even after the French government had been apprised of the colonial government's inability to handle the influx.

Joining in the migration were significant numbers of Acadians whose initial reticence was gradually worn down by pressure from Choiseul and their local intendants who, by 1765, were offering, in the king's name, increased inducements for resettlement. On June 21, 1763, for example, Sieur Mistral, intendant at Le Havre, was authorized to send to the colony "five or six . . . settlers from North America" (*i.e.*, Acadian exiles) per departing vessel and to pay the ship outfitters a bounty of 100 *livres* for each North American passenger.[126] Acadian historian Emile Lauvrière estimates that "several hundred"

Acadians made their way from France's Atlantic seaports to Cayenne. In April 1765 alone, approximately twenty-four Acadian families are known to have left Morlaix for French Guiana. Undetermined numbers of exiles from other French seaports are known to have followed, as well as approximately 100 Acadians who sailed from Miquelon for Cayenne in late October 1765.[127]

The Acadian colonists, like their fellow travellers, soon had ample cause to regret their decision. Like the Germans, the Acadians spent weeks, sometimes months, awaiting transportation to settlement sites. Living in overcrowded and unsanitary temporary housing, many of these new colonists contracted various diseases and died before ever seeing their promised land grants.

The settlers' difficulties stemmed in no small part from the colonial governor's malfeasance. Although allocated sufficient funds and invested with sufficient authority to deal with the problem of massive European immigration, Governor Turgot remained in France—with his governmental funds—until late December 1764, and, upon arrival, ignored the problems of the settlers, choosing instead to squander his budget upon lavish banquets for administrators at the colonial capital. Meanwhile, *Commissaire-ordonnateur* Chanvallon, chief of the colonial bureaucracy who had accompanied the first colonists to Guiana, had been forced to grapple with the immigrants' day-to-day problems without adequate financial resources. In fact, by the end of 1763, he had been compelled to operate the government with 172,274 *livres* borrowed from the colonists. However, private loans, even in such significant amounts, could not meet the needs of the swelling tide of immigrants which, by the end of 1765, reportedly had swelled to more than 9,000.

Given its fiscal constraints, the Guiana government, during the height of the influx in 1763 and 1764, could do little more than erect hundreds of hovels to provide temporary housing and construct makeshift hospitals to care for hundreds of colonists.[128] The effort to provide even these limited facilities quickly proved overwhelming as the stream of immigration grew into a torrent. By June 1764, the colony's primitive hospital contained 800 patients, while several hundred convalescents required additional care. Similarly, the demand for temporary housing quickly outstripped Chanvallon's ability to provide it. In 1764, 2,300 immigrants were forced by these circumstances to land at Devil's Island where, in the absence of any facilities, they "died like flies" of "fevers, scurvy, malnutrition, and dehydration."[129]

The demands of dealing with these crises diverted resources which would ordinarily have been used to settle the immigrants, thus compounding the *commissaire-ordonnateur*'s seemingly insurmountable problems. By June 1764, the colony's administrative chief was forced to restrict rations intended for all settlers to hospital patients. The need to constantly expand the hospital and to construct temporary shelters also left Chanvallon few workers with which to relocate able-bodied colonists. In 1763, even before the onset of massive immigration, government employees had staked out only forty-four concessions (land grants) in the jungle lining the lower Kouru River and, on each concession, had erected four palmetto "posts" to indicate the four corners of the dwelling to be constructed there. Settlers were subsequently deposited on these land grants, given modest supplies of provisions and tools, and then abandoned. In late 1763, 1764, and 1765, fewer and fewer colonists received even this token assistance.

Thus confronted with diminishing prospects for resettlement and increasing prospects for sickness and death, thousands of Guiana colonists, including most—if not all—of the Acadian survivors, returned to France, most arriving at the port of Saint-Jean-d'Angély in 1765. The tales of these penniless and dejected veterans of Guiana colonization helped stem the flow of Acadian emigration. By the late 1780s, only one Acadian family remained in Guiana, but the 1794 census of that colony lists no Acadian surnames.[130]

Falkland Islands[131]

While some Acadians pondered the merits of Guiana colonization in 1763 and 1764, other exiles were setting sail for the Falkland Islands. At the beginning of 1763, Louis Antoine de Bougainville, a distinguished French military officer and

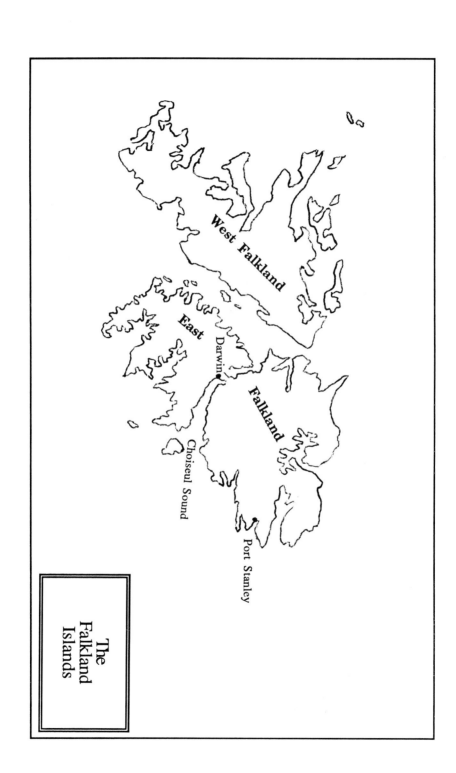

West Falkland

East

Falkland

Darwin

Choiseul Sound

Port Stanley

The
Falkland
Islands

explorer, requested and obtained French governmental authorization to establish a colony on the Falklands at personal expense.[132] Louis XV also authorized the Acadians in France to participate in the proposed colonization venture, noting that they would continue to receive their daily dole (6 *sols*) throughout the duration of the expidition. Despite this inducement to participate, only two Acadian families[133] apparently expressed any interest.[134] When Bougainville sailed from St. Malo, France, on September 15, 1763, with two ships (the *Aigle* and the *Sphinx*), only nine Acadian colonists were aboard. After stopping at Montevideo to purchase livestock for the colony, Bougainville's expedition landed at East Falkland Island on February 3, 1764, and, on March 17, 1764, the colonists quickly set about establishing Fort Saint-Louis,[135] a post on Berkeley Sound.[136] On April 5, 1764, Bougainville took possession of the islands, which he christened Malouines in honor of St. Malo, in the name of Louis XV.[137] The successful establishment of this colony and the simultaneous collapse of the Guiana colonization effort, caused the Acadians in France to see Bougainville's venture in a new light.

This change in attitude was not lost upon the French government; on August 6, 1764, the naval ministry authorized Bougainville, who had recently returned to France to acquire provisions and additional colonists for the Falkland outpost, to recruit "eighty to one hundred" St. Malo Acadians. Bougainville again approached the exiles, and, armed with ministerial assurances that Acadian colonists would continue to receive their customary dole and that they would, in addition, receive rations for one year after their arrival, his overtures proved remarkably persuasive.[138] Eighty additional settlers— all Acadians from St. Malo—arrived in April 1765, increasing the colony's population to 150. A third contingent of seventy-nine colonists, most of whom were Acadians, arrived in 1766.[139]

The establishment of a permanent French colony on the Falklands elicited an outcry from the British and Spanish governments, both of which saw the islands as a potentially strategic naval base.[140] To solidify British claims to the island, Commodore John Byron, then engaged in gathering military intelligence in the South Atlantic aboard two naval vessels, landed on East Falkland Island on January 11, 1765, and claimed the island for Britian. Apparently unaware of Fort Saint-Louis's existence, Byron notified King George III that he had taken possession of unoccupied territory. The British government subsequently dispatched Captain John McBride to establish Port Egmont, an outpost on West Falkland Island manned by twenty-five soldiers. Learning on March 17, 1766, of the existence of a French settlement in the Falklands, McBride set out to locate the colonists, whom he incorrectly believed to be incursionists. While surveying the Falkland Islands, on December 4, 1766, McBride encountered the French settlement on East Falkland and, after demanding to see Bougainville's royal letter of authorization, ordered the Fort Saint-Louis colonists to evacuate the island or face a military invasion.[141]

Meanwhile, the Spanish government, which learned of the French colony's existence from Spanish authorities at Montevideo, filed an official protest with the French government. Spain claimed title to the islands on the basis of their "proximity" to the South American mainland, which had been ceded to Spain through the Treaty of Tordesillas (1494). To avoid any confrontation with its military ally, however, Spain offered to reimburse the French for any expenses incurred in establishing the Fort Saint-Louis settlement. Equally unwilling to jeopardize the Family Compact binding France and Spain, the French government was compelled to accept the Spanish offer. Bougainville was duly ordered to negotiate a price with the Spanish crown and then to transfer possession of the Falklands to a Spanish representative. After accepting a "liberal sum" at Madrid in 1766,[142] Bougainville sailed to Montevideo, arriving there on January 31, 1767. After subsequently stopping at Buenos Airies to rendezvous with Spanish authorities assigned to take possession of the French colony, Bougainville sailed to Fort Saint-Louis, arriving there on March 25. On April 1, Bougainville transferred the colony to Spain. During the transfer ceremony, Bougainville "read the King's letter to the French [*i.e.* Acadian] inhabitants of this infant colony, by which his Majesty [Louis XV] permits their remaining under the government of his Most Catholic Majesty [the Spanish king]."[143] Bougainville noted that "some families [numbering approximately ninety-five individuals][144] profited of this permission, the rest, with the garrison embarked on board the Spanish frigates which sailed for Montevideo, [on] the 27th in the morning."[145]   At this juncture, the Falkland Acadians temporarily fade from the documentary record. Bougainville's correspondence indicates only that he had entrusted an undetermined number of sick, departing exiles to the care of the Spanish governor at Buenos Aires.[146]   Whether or not they received the necessary care is uncertain.   It is also unclear whether the departing Acadians continued their journey to France via Montevideo, or whether they were forced to remain temporarily in the Uruguayan port following their arrival there.

Nor is the fate of the few Acadians remaining on the Falklands clearly set out. It is certain, however, that the life of the Acadians remaining on the island was difficult. Colonel Catani, commander of the Spanish garrison stationed on the islands, complained of the wretched condition of the "huts" in which the settlers lived, while Felipe Ruiz Puente, first Spanish governor of the Falklands, informed his superiors that corn would not grow and that gardens could be made to produce only with great difficulty, and only if high walls were built around them to protect them from the continuous winds. Cattle prospered on the islands, but few cattle had been introduced by Bougainville,[147] forcing the colonists to engage in seal hunting, at least on a limited basis.[148] Given these circumstances, plus the continuous threat of Anglo-Hispanic hostilities, it seems unlikely that the remaining Acadians would have settled permanently on the Falklands. As late as 1785, the Spanish colony on the Falklands boasted a civilian population of less than 100, indicating a slow decline in population.[149] Publications on the Acadian experience in the Falklands note only that an undetermined number of Acadians subsequently made their way back to France in a "more or less miserable state."   Ministerial correspondence in France's Archives Nationales records the arrival of at least three groups of Acadian stragglers from the south Atlantic—in July 1769; June 1771; and May 1775.[150]

St. Pierre and Miquelon[151]

While the Guiana and Falkland colonization attempts were underway, the exiles were colonizing St. Pierre and Miquelon, which, for many Acadians, provided the nearest refuge from British oppression. Though it enjoyed the full support of the exiles, this venture proved only marginally more successful than those in which the Acadians were reluctant participants.

The Acadian migration to St. Pierre and Miquelon began in 1758, as a small number of Cape Breton Acadians fled the English occupation of their homeland.[152] Large-scale Acadian immigration, however, would not begin until 1763. The Treaty of Paris, ratified on February 10, 1763, granted the Acadians exiled to British possessions an eighteen-month grace period in which to relocate on French soil. The treaty also established St. Pierre and Miquelon as the only remaining French possessions in North America. Hundreds of exiles from New England, Prince Edward Island, and Nova Scotia consequently began to converge on these islands, apparently with the intention of remaining there until circumstances should permit them to return to their homes. Between 1763 and 1767, they were joined by hundreds of Acadians fleeing their impoverished circumstances in the French Atlantic cities[153]

The Acadian migration to St. Pierre and Miquelon caused the French government a great deal of concern. The dearth of wood and sterile soil on the islands prevented the immigrants from supporting themselves by traditional agricultural means, and fishing, which offered a perennial bounty, was capable of supporting only a relatively small population. Knowing of the Acadian desire for reunification and the financial and logistical problems which their reunification on St. Pierre and Miquelon would entail, and fearing that the British would come to view the colony as a military threat if large numbers of hostile Acadians were massed on the islands near British Newfoundland, the French government directed Sieur Dangeac,[154] first governor of the islands, to discourage immigration. In his instructions, issued on February 27, 1763, Dangeac was authorized to support only three hundred Acadian immigrants, whom he was permitted to take with him aboard the

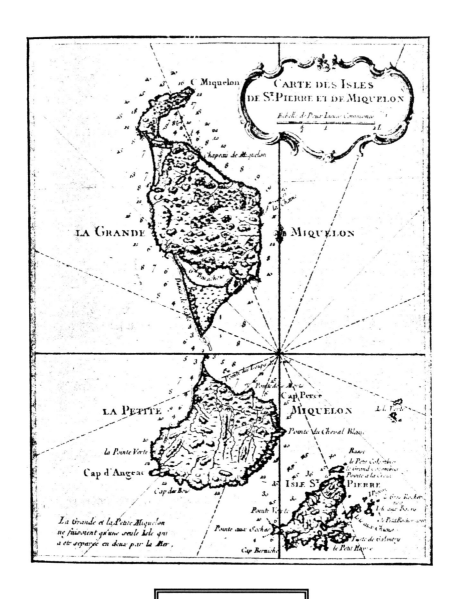

St. Pierre and
Miquelon,
ca. 1770

Garonne, soon to be sailing from Rochefort naval yard.[155] He was, in addition, directed to purchase large quantities of fishing equipment, to be dispensed upon arrival to make the colonists more self sufficient.

Dangeac's instructions and his efforts to make the nascent colony self-supporting were for naught, for Acadians on both sides of the Atlantic ignored and migrated to the islands in large numbers: One hundred and sixteen exiles from Boston reached Miquelon on October 1, 1763. Another one hundred Acadians from Chédabouctou, the Isthmus of Chignecto, Prince Edward Island, and Cape Breton Island—all of whom had been imprisoned in different Nova Scotian forts during the twilight years of the Seven Years' War—sailed to Miquelon in August 1764 after refusing to take the oath of allegiance to Britain necessary for them to remain in their homeland. One hundred and eleven Acadians from Prince Edward Island and Halifax, Nova Scotia made their way to Miquelon around October 2, 1765, while seventy-two other Acadians from Beauséjour arrived approximately two weeks later.[156] Their numbers were augmented by approximately fifty Acadians who sailed with the French fishing fleet to the Grand Banks and who jumped ship at St. Pierre.

Dangeac attempted to discourage each group of immigrants from remaining in the colony. Instead, he and French recruiting agents encouraged the exiles to migrate to Cayenne or Guiana, but, in each instance, his urgings fell on deaf ears. Indeed, Dangeac reported on October 4, 1764, that "they had been unable to persuade a single Acadian to go to this climate which terrifies them."[157] Thus forced to deal with the needs of these unwanted colonists, Dangeac utilized his very limited resources to erect crude housing for each wave of immigrants. Built of spruce stakes planted in the ground, covered with sod, and warmed by chimneys made of mud, clay and hay, these structures provided meagre protection from the elements; the problem of inadequate housing was solved by the colonists who gradually improved their accommodations. But other problems were not so easily solved, including the islands' rapidly dwindling supply of wood, the difficulty experienced by Acadian farmers in adapting to deep-sea fishing, and the colony's increasingly severe supply shortages. The last two problems were particularly significant, for as late as June 1767, 103 Acadian families numbering 551 individuals were still living on government rations. As a result, by 1765, a sense of impending doom pervaded the now demoralized Acadian community.[158]

These fears were realized in the mid-to-late 1760s. In mid-November 1765, Dangeac, who was no longer able to feed and house all of the incoming immigrants, was forced to send to Nantes forty-three of the seventy-two Acadian refugees who had reached Miquelon only weeks earlier.[159]

The supply shortages which forced the aforementioned Acadians to emigrate to France compelled the French government to intervene to relieve the overcrowding on St. Pierre and Miquelon. Citing the French government's inability to maintain so large a population on lands "completely devoid of resources," the president of the French Council of Marine notified Dangeac, on behalf of Louis XV, that the unauthorized Acadian settlers must either return to Acadia or to go to France, where they would receive the same modest benefits extended to the exiles already in the motherland. This announcement, made apparently the following spring, generated a great deal of consternation among the Acadians. According to Dangeac:

> We told them the king's wishes, and asked if they wished to go to France or return to Acadia. This proposition caused them the greatest consternation, each having expended its meagre resources in building a house and making a garden. They actually have twelve schooners and ten fishing skiffs. They are attached to France and do not wish to return to Acadia. Several among them would gladly go to Louisiana if we wished to transport them there.[160]

The Acadians' wishes notwithstanding, no government-subsidized transportation to Louisiana was forthcoming, nor would it be for a generation. Indeed, only fourteen of the Miquelonnais would ever reach Louisiana, apparently as part of the 1785 migration.[161] As Dangeac predicted, most of the Acadians slated for deportation consequently decided to cast their lot with France. According to historian Michel Poirier, 763 persons—nearly all of whom were Acadians—left St. Pierre and Miquelon between October and late December 1767. Of this number 586 sailed to France, while 163 went to Acadia. Most of the latter settled at Cape Breton Island, Ile Madame, and Cocagne, in present-day New Brunswick.[162]

Following the return of the Acadians to France, merchants with a vested interest in maintaining the colony's larger population base began petitioning the minister of Marine to reverse his decision, arguing that a larger colony could be self-supporting if the inhabitants were all forced to engage in fishing. The merchants' petitions were reinforced by petitions from 240 Acadians in Rochefort and St. Malo urging the ministry to reconsider the existing, government-imposed, demographic limitations on their adopted homeland.[163] In a rare display of vacillation, Choiseul reversed his decision in early 1768 and conditionally approved a limited migration of the displaced Miquelonnais to the islands they had only recently departed. The Acadians returning to St. Pierre and Miquelon, however, were required to be fully self-supporting and to provide their own transportation.

Utilizing two Acadian-owned schooners aboard which they had travelled to France in 1767, the Rochefort Acadians began to retrace their steps to Miquelon during the spring of 1768. The first immigrants—thirty-seven persons sailing aboard the *Créole*—reached their destination on May 5, 1768. They were followed on June 23 by sixty-six Acadians aboard the *Louise*. An additional 219 exiles disembarked at Miquelon after Choiseul again reversed himself and granted the immigrants free passage aboard a royal supply vessel.[164]

Once reestablished on the islands, the Acadian population endured, once again, the rigors of life in an increasingly marginal environment, which annually afforded the struggling settlers fewer resources. In an effort to become more self-sufficient, the exiles introduced livestock, but this experiment failed. According to Joseph Woodmass, a representative of the Nova Scotian government who toured St. Pierre and Miquelon in 1769, the Acadians, upon their return from France, found only a few "skinny cows, the sheep and lambs brought from France [having] died of starvation."[165] Many Miquelonnais, the Nova Scotia representative maintained, feared that, without governmental assistance, they would share the fate of the sheep. In fact, the situation had become so bleak by late 1769 that several Acadians, who had been detained at Halifax during the Seven Years' War, secretly requested passports to Nova Scotia from Woodmass.[166]

The lives of the St. Pierre and Miquelon settlers gradually improved as markets for Miquelon codfish developed in France and in the Antilles. Between 1766 and 1778, 718 ships transported nearly a half-million quintals of salted cod to the metropole and the Caribbean.[167] Economic growth produced a corresponding increase in the Acadian population. In 1776, St. Pierre and Miquelon boasted a population of 1,894.[168]

The growing economic and demographic significance of St. Pierre and Miquelon made the islands a tempting military target. Following France's declaration of war against England on February 6, 1778,[169] British naval forces from Newfoundland invaded the islands and laid to waste the Acadian settlements there. In scenes reminiscent of the deportations of 1755, the inhabitants of St. Pierre and Miquelon were forced aboard vessels, without being given time "to even save their clothes," while soldiers went from house to house, burning the structures and their contents. Once again, the Miquelonnais were forced to sail to France.[170]

Dispersed during the crossing, the refugees landed at Nantes, La Rochelle, Rochefort, Cherbourg, and St. Malo. Unable to return to their homes for the duration of the American Revolution, these Acadians, who had been driven from their homes for the third time in a generation, were forced, once again, to live on the French dole. After promulgation of the Treaty of Paris ending the war for independence in May 1783, approximately 1,250 Acadians petititioned the French government for permission to return to St. Pierre and Miquelon. According to published sources, 510 Acadians made the crossing in 1783, followed by an additional 713 in 1784. Using lumber removed from the French Shore of Newfoundland, they quickly rebuilt their settlements and reestablished the local cod industry, which attracted hundreds of

Acadians and Frenchmen from the continent as seasonal workers each summer.[171]

The colony's renewed success again marked it for invasion. On May 14, 1793, during the Anglo-French hostilities precipitated by the French Revolution, a small British army invaded Miquelon and, on June 20, deported the island's tiny French garrison and its non-resident fishermen to Halifax. Unable to support these prisoners, the Nova Scotian government sent them to France, where groups of them arrived between June and late September 1794.[172]

After a failed attempt to get the resident fishermen to work as fishermen for the British, the invaders also expelled the remaining Acadians from Miquelon and St. Pierre. This time, the soldiers' work was made easier by the voluntary flight of numerous settlers. Anticipating another deportation, approximately thirty-two Acadian families fled to the Iles Madeleine, establishing the first settlements there in 1793. Another 360 Acadians migrated to Ile Madame.[173] Those who remained, however, were placed aboard British vessels on September 14, 1796, and sent to Halifax, from which they were sent to various fishing villages and forced to work on English fishing vessels in the Grand Banks. Only on July 23, 1796, after the provincial government was convinced that they "could derive no further advantage" from the exiles, did the governor of Nova Scotia heed the Acadian demand for repatriation to France.[174] Vessels carrying the latest Acadian exiles reached Bordeaux in July 1797 and Le Havre in August 1797.[175]

Undeterred by their seemingly unending tale of woe, hundreds of these refugees and their descendants would return to St. Pierre and Miquelon following the cessation of Anglo-French hostilities through the 1814 Treaty of Paris. By 1820, 800 Acadians had become permanent residents of the islands.[176]

Louisiana[177]

At the time of the initial St. Pierre and Miquelon colonization attempt, some Acadians also looked to Louisiana for resettlement. In September, 1766, one Semer, an Acadian residing at Le Havre, received a letter from his son, Jean-

Baptiste, who had recently settled at the Attakapas post in Louisiana. The younger Semer described Louisiana in glowing terms and his father spread reports of his son's good fortune throughout the communities of exiles in France. France, which had transferred western Louisiana, including the Attakapas post, to Spain in 1763, refused to subsidize a migration of Acadians to Louisiana. The Acadians thus remained marooned in France until 1785, when the Spanish government, acting through Henri Peyroux de la Coudrenière, a French soldier of fortune recently returned from Louisiana, and Olivier Terrio (Theriot), recruited approximately 1,600 Acadians for resettlement in Spain's sprawling Mississippi Valley colony.

The Acadians in France, however, merely constituted the last major wave of French immigration to the Mississippi Valley. The first Acadians to reach Louisiana following ratification of the Treaty of Paris were twenty individuals from New York.[178] This group included Acadians deported to New York in 1755 and relatives recently released from detention camps at Fort Edward, Nova Scotia. Arriving at New Orleans in early April 1764, they were settled by Louisiana's caretaker French administration along the Mississippi River above New Orleans, near the boundary between present-day St. John and St. James parishes.[179]

These immigrants were followed, in late February 1765, by 193 Acadian refugees from detention camps at Halifax.[180] These Acadians initially sought to relocate at Saint-Domingue, the French sugar island to which approximately 2,000 of their confrères had fled in late 1763 and early 1764. The refugees from the mainland, however, quickly discovered that life in the Antilles was far more difficult than it had been under English dominion: Acadians were impressed into work details and sent to build the Môle St-Nicolas naval base in the midst of a jungle. The workers were unpaid, receiving as compensation for their labors discarded clothing and inadequate supplies. Their children quickly succumbed to the twin scourges of malnutrition and disease (usually scurvy), while they and their wives fell victim to the climate and indemic fevers. Those Acadians who survived were generally unable to find an

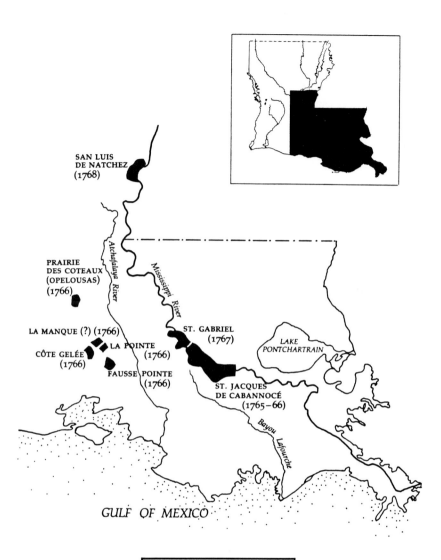

SAN LUIS
DE NATCHEZ
(1768)

PRAIRIE
DES COTEAUX
(OPELOUSAS)
(1766)

LA MANQUE (?) (1766)

CÔTE GELÉE
(1766)

LA POINTE
(1766)

FAUSSE POINTE
(1766)

Atchafalaya River

Mississippi River

ST. GABRIEL
(1767)

*LAKE
PONTCHARTRAIN*

ST. JACQUES
DE CABANNOCÉ
(1765–66)

Bayou Lafourche

GULF OF MEXICO

Acadian
Settlements
in
Spanish
Louisiana

economic niche in the island's plantation economy, which offered few opportunities to independent farmers.[181]

As the Halifax Acadians prepared to migrate to the French Antilles, letters from Saint-Domingue reached them carrying reports of maltreatment by French colonial authorities.[182] Repelled by substandard food and clothing, tropical diseases, and social and economic incompatibility with the island's plantation economy, the Saint-Domingue Acadians resolved to migrate en masse to French-speaking Quebec via the Mississippi Valley, and they invited their cousins in Halifax to join them.[183] Incredible as it may seem, extant sources in Halifax indicate that local Acadians, driven to desperation by the recent reports from Saint-Domingue and by the British government's rejection of their efforts to be settled in Canada, embraced this ambitious scheme. Indeed, the Halifax Acadians reportedly anticipated the creation of a major Acadian settlement in Illinois.[184]

Their dreams were never realized. Although the Halifax Acadians chartered a boat for Saint-Domingue, they subsequently discovered that the vast majority of their confrères were either dead or destitute and unable to afford passage to Louisiana.[185] The Halifax Acadians, led by the legendary Joseph Broussard *dit* Beausoleil, were thus forced to change ships and continue on alone to the Mississippi Valley.[186] Arriving at New Orleans in late February 1765 with little more than the clothes they carried on their backs, 193 Halifax Acadians were greeted by a colonial government nearly as destitute as they. Louisiana had been partitioned by the Treaty of Paris (1763) into English and Spanish sectors. Anticipating expeditious occupation of the trans-Appalachian and trans-Mississippi regions respectively by British and Spanish authorities, the French government failed to send material assistance and provisions to Louisiana after 1763.[187] Moved by pity, Louisiana's French caretaker administrators nevertheless mobilized what limited resources were available, providing each family with land grants, seed grain for six months, a gun, and crude land-clearing implements. The Louisiana government also provided a former military engineer, Louis Andry, to conduct them to the Attakapas

District, a frontier post selected for their settlement, and to supervise their establishment.[188]

Though thus thwarted in their efforts to reach the Upper Mississippi Valley, subsequently harassed by the Attakapas commandant, and decimated by either malaria or yellow fever in the summer and fall of 1765, the Halifax Acadians survived these calamities and, by dint of their unstinting industry, soon prospered.[189] Antonio de Ulloa, Louisiana's first Spanish governor who arrived at New Orleans on March 5, 1766, stood in awe of his newly established Acadian subjects, who, he observed, literally worked themselves to death to provide for their destitute families as well as their orphaned and widowed relatives. Their persistent labors quickly transformed the region's semi-tropical jungles into productive farms, and within a decade the exiles enjoyed a standard of living at least equal to that of their predispersal homeland. The Attakapas Acadians were clearly sustained in their herculean tasks by a desire to create a new homeland not only for themselves but also for their displaced friends and relatives. Thus, when Ulloa toured the Acadian settlements along Bayou Teche in late spring 1766, the Attakapas settlers sought permission to invite their relatives remaining in exile to join in their good fortune.[190] By this means, the Attakapas Acadians sought to reunite their scattered families in their adopted home, which they now proudly called "New Acadia."

When Ulloa equivocated, citing the necessity of securing royal authorization, the immigrants characteristically ignored the governor's pleas to desist and in 1766 and 1767 numerous letters of invitation from Attakapas Acadians were circulating widely among the Acadians remaining in exile in Maryland and, later, in Pennsylvania.[191] Pooling their meagre resources to charter local merchant vessels for Louisiana, hundreds of Acadians—at least 689 of the 1,050 known survivors in Maryland and Pennsylvania—boarded vessels in Chesapeake Bay ports for Louisiana.[192] Arriving at New Orleans, these refugees were greeted as cordially as their predecessors and were offered land and material assistance to facilitate their establishment.[193] Amicable relations between the immigrants and their Spanish hosts soured, however, as a bitter dispute arose in 1767 and 1768 over the new Acadian settlement sites. No objections had been voiced when at least 200 Maryland Acadians had been sent to Cabannocé (present-day St. James Parish) and later to Ascension Parish in the fall of 1766.[194] The caretaker French government had been compelled by circumstances to settle approximately 80 late-arriving Halifax Acadians at Cabannocé in May 1765, and the proximity of the new settlement sites to those of 1765 seemed to portend at least partial realization of the Acadian dream of familial reunificaion.[195] However, the subsequent waves of Maryland and Pennsylvania Acadians were forcibly dispersed, in conformity with Spanish defensive strategy. Extremely concerned about the vulnerability of Louisiana's eastern frontier to Indian and British encroachment and lacking the troops necessary to protect its extensive borders, Ulloa decided, in May 1766, to employ the immigrants in the colonial defenses. After May 1766, each wave of immigrants was assigned to a strategic site along the Mississippi River which constituted the international boundary between British and Spanish territory. Although the Acadian settlement sites were sometimes isolated and vulnerable to attack, Ulloa hoped that the marksmanship and virulent anglophobia of the immigrants would make the new river posts an adequate first line of defense in the event of Anglo-Hispanic hostilities. Thus, in July 1767, 210 Acadians were assigned to Fort St. Gabriel, while in February 1768, 149 immigrants were ordered to San Luis de Natchez, near present-day Vidalia, Louisiana.[196]

The dispersal of the immigrants earned the Spanish government the enmity of the Acadian community which, by 1768,[197] had emerged as the predominant cultural group in Lower Louisiana, outside New Orleans and its immediate environs. As a result, the Acadians became active participants in the ouster of Ulloa during the New Orleans rebellion of 1768.[198] Marching into New Orleans on the morning of Oct. 29, 1768, scores of exiles (perhaps as many as 200-300) took up arms to force the Spanish governor's unceremonious departure from Louisiana.

Spanish control over the colony was restored in August 1769. As a conciliatory gesture, Alejandro O'Reilly, Ulloa's successor as governor, permitted the disgruntled San Luis de Natchez settlers to migrate to the Acadian settlements along the Mississippi River in late December 1769. This judicious move did much to placate the colony's Acadian population. But Hispano-Acadian friction and the instability during and following the October 1768 insurrection seems to have discouraged further Acadian immigration into Louisiana. Indeed, while it is possible that a handful of individuals may have found their way to the colony in ensuing years, only one small group of Acadians is known to have arrived in Louisiana between 1768 and 1785. In 1770, a haggard band of 30 Acadians arrived at Natchitoches, Louisiana after a fifteen-month ordeal of shipboard starvation, mutiny, shipwreck, imprisonment and forced labor in Spanish Texas, and finally a 420-mile overland trek to Louisiana. After successfully resisting government efforts to settle them permanently in the Natchitoches post, these refugees established homes first in the Iberville district and later at Opelousas.[199]

TABLE VI
ACADIAN MIGRATIONS TO LOUISIANA,
1764-1788

Place of Origin	Date	Number of Exiles
New York	1764	20
Halifax	1764-1765	311?
Maryland & Pennsylvania	1766-1770	689?
France	1785	1,596
St. Pierre/Miquelon	1788	19
TOTAL		2,635?

The arrival of these immigrants marked the end of the Acadian influx from the Atlantic seaboard colonies. The next wave of Acadian immigration emanated from France, but, once again, Louisiana influences served as the catalyst for the migration. In 1766, letters from Attakapas Acadians to relatives in France had much the same impact as they had had earlier on their counterparts in Maryland.[200] Indeed, the approximately 2,500 Acadian refugees in France endured conditions at least as bad, and in some cases, worse than those suffered by the exiles in English captivity.[201] But Acadians in France lacked the resources to take advantage of the opportunity to seek a better life in Lower Louisiana, and the financially embarrassed French government refused to subsidize their relocation as it would benefit only the Spanish crown.[202]

Thus forced to remain in France and to endure several disastrous resettlement programs in succeeding years, the Acadians maintained their interest in Louisiana through a steady flow of correspondence that crossed the Atlantic in the 1760s, 1770s, and early 1780s.[203] Though none of these letters has survived, numerous references to them in Louisiana, French, and Spanish colonial archives indicate that many, perhaps most, Louisiana Acadians managed somehow to contact their displaced relatives overseas and, by extolling the virtues of the Mississippi Valley's salubrious climate, fertile soil, and abundant unclaimed lands, enticed them to rejoin their kinsmen in the new Acadian homeland. Indeed, the volume of Acadian correspondence reached such proportions that in 1767 exiles at Belle-Isle-en-Mer, France, could describe accurately the location and status of literally hundreds of relatives in St. Pierre and Miquelon, Quebec Province, the Maritimes, the thirteen English seaboard colonies, and Louisiana. These letters helped to keep alive the spark of interest in Louisiana colonization among the Acadians in France, and this continuing interest was successfully exploited in 1784 by Henri Peyroux de la Coudrenière, a French soldier of fortune recently returned from Louisiana, whose Spanish government was actively seeking colonists. By providing colonists for Louisiana, Peyroux anticipated a handsome reward from a grateful Spanish monarch. Working through Acadian shoemaker Olivier Terrio (Theriot), Peyroux gradually overcame the initial Acadian incredulity and the subsequent resistance of the French government in organizing the largest single migration of Europeans into the Mississippi Valley in the late eighteenth-century. Between mid-May and mid-October 1785, 1,596 Acadians boarded seven New Orleans-bound merchant vessels chartered at various French ports by the

Spanish government for their transportation.[204]

Upon arrival at New Orleans, the 1785 immigrants were housed in converted warehouses on the western riverbank. While recuperating from the deleterious effects of their trans-Atlantic voyage, they selected delegates to inspect potential home sites in Lower Louisiana. On the basis of their representatives' reports, the exiles selected, on an individual basis, the most appealing settlement. Individual interests, however, were usually subordinated to those of the group, as eighty-four percent of the immigrants endorsed the sites recommended by their delegates. Four of the seven groups of passengers elected to establish communities along Bayou Lafourche, settling between present-day Labadieville and Raceland.[205] Two other contingents of French Acadians selected lands along the Mississippi River near Baton Rouge.[206] The final group of immigrants accepted lands along lower Bayou des Ecores (present-day Thompson's Creek); this group was later forced to relocate along Bayou Lafourche when a 1794 hurricane unleashed torrential rains that literally washed away their farms.[207]

The resettlement of the Bayou des Ecores Acadians marked the final episode of the major Acadian migration to Louisiana in the late eighteenth century. Only nineteen Acadian refugees from St. Pierre Island, Canada, who arrived at New Orleans in 1788 aboard Capt. Joseph Gravois's schooner, are known to have reached the colony between 1785 and 1800. There were also an undetermined, but small, number of Acadians among the 10,000 Saint-Domingue refugees who arrived en masse at New Orleans in the fall of 1809. The evidence suggests, however, that these latter-day immigrants were few in number and that they had already lost much, if not all, of their ethnic identity.[208] Thus, when forced by circumstances to remain in New Orleans, the Acadian refugees were quickly amalgamated into the Crescent City's flourishing Creole culture.

Conclusion

The Saint-Domingue influx marked the final chapter in the Acadian exiles. In the course of these wanderings, the

Acadians established two new homelands—one in present-day New Brunswick, the other in Louisiana—both of which they christened "New Acadia." Though widely separated, environmentally dissimilar, and subject to different European governments, both sanctuaries served their intended functions: They provided the demographic critical mass necessary for survival. Only in these havens, and in small, isolated satellite settlements near them, would the Acadian people maintain their identity. Acadians unable or unwilling to make their way to the major Acadian colonies were very quickly swallowed up by their host cultures, and thousands of modern-day Québecois, Frenchmen, and New Englanders are completely oblivious to their biological ties to the Acadian exiles.

Even in the new Acadian homelands, economic, cultural, demographic, and environmental factors slowly transformed the transplanted peoples. Environmental factors were the most immediate and compelling catalysts for change. In New Brunswick, the sterile, rocky soil of the northern coastal region forced the former farmers to seek their livelihood as fishermen, while Louisiana's subtropical environment imposed different, but equally radical, economic changes.

The cultural landscapes of the two new Acadian homelands were equally dissimilar. While the undisputed demographic and cultural kingpins in their original settlement sites, the transplanted Acadian communities saw their hegemonic positions rapidly eroded through massive, non-Acadian immigration. Within a century of their reestablishment, the Acadian communities of New Brunswick and Louisiana were reduced to minority status, even within their native counties/parishes. Though relations between the Acadians and their neighbors were frequently less than harmoneous, mutual cultural interaction born of economic necessity gradually transformed both Acadian communities. Yet, there remained, and remains to this day, sufficient shared traits to produce an immediate cultural bond between Acadians of all geographic areas, a bond that bridges the gaps of time and space caused by the Acadian diaspora.

NOTES

*This study was made possible in part through financial support from the Jean Lafitte National Park, New Orleans, Louisiana.

[1] For the best estimates of the northern Acadian population in the modern period, see Muriel K. Roy, "Settlement and Population Growth in Acadia," in Jean Daigle, ed., *The Acadians of the Maritimes* (Moncton, N.B., 1982), p. 167.

[2] In the 1970s, Canadian demographers had come up with a figure as inflated as many of the present estimates of the Acadian populations in Louisiana and the Canadian Maritimes—23,000,000! Interview with Jean Daigle, then director of the Centre d'Etudes Acadiennes at the Université de Moncton, Moncton, Nouveau Brunswick, Canada, at New Iberia, Louisiana, October, 1977.

[3] Carl A. Brasseaux, *The Founding of New Acadia: The Beginnings of Acadian Life in Louisiana, 1765-1803* (Baton Rouge, 1987), pp. 13-24.

[4] Edouard Richard, *Acadia: Missing Links of a Lost Chapter in American History*, 2 vols. (New York, 1895), I, 220-224, 319; John Bartlet Brebner, *New England's Outpost: Acadia Before the Conquest*, (New York, 1927), p. 127.

[5] Naomi Griffiths, *The Acadians: Creation of a People*, (Toronto, 1973), pp. 46, 49-51; Brebner, *New England's Outpost*, pp. 176, 183; Richard, *Acadia*, I, 355-356.

[6] For the best discussion of the debate over the size of the pre-dispersal Acadian population, see Daigle, ed., *The Acadians of the Maritimes*, pp. 134-156.

[7] This remarkable rate persisted despite a 28 percent infant mortality rate and a 50 percent child mortality rate. Griffiths, *Creation of a People*, p. 14; Andrew Hill Clark, *Acadia: The Geography of Early Nova Scotia to 1760*, (Madison, Wis., 1968), pp. 99-100, 121-131, 201-212.

[8] Emile Lauvrière, *La Tragédie d'un peuple: Le drame du peuple acadien*, 2 vols. (Paris, 1932), I, 307-313, 387-395, 410; Thomas Beamish Akins, ed., *Acadie and Nova Scotia: Documents Relating to the Acadian French and the First British Colonization of the Province, 1714-1758*, (Cottonport, La., 1972), pp. 234-376, 391, 409; Brebner, *New England's Outpost*, p. 209; Richard, *Acadia*, I, 217-226.

[9] Griffiths, *Creation of a People*, p. 54; Akins, ed., *Acadia and Nova Scotia*, p. 258, 263-267.

[10] Lauvrière, *Tragédie*, I, 396-397, 446, 448-449, 455-459, 484; Akins, ed., *Acadia and Nova Scotia*, pp. 267-269.

[11] Lauvrière, *Tragédie*, I, 456-459, 464, 471-472, 482-483.

[12] *Ibid.*

[13] *Ibid.*, I, 479, 484-493.

[14] Clark, *Acadia*, p. 346.

[15] See Robert LeBlanc, "The Acadian Migrations," *Proceedings of the Minnesota*

Academy of Science, XXX (1962), pp. 15; Milton P. Rieder and Norma Gaudet Rieder, comps., *The Acadian Exiles in the American Colonies, 1755-1768.* Metairie, La., 1977; Janet Jehn, comp., *Acadian Exiles in the Colonies* (Covington, Ky., 1977).

[16]Lawrence Henry Gipson, *The British Empire Before the American Revolution,* 15 vols. (New York, 1946-1970), VI, 283.

[17]*Ibid.,* VI, 286-344.

[18]*Ibid.,* pp. 287-88; John Reynolds to the British Board of Trade, April 16, 1758, Public Record Office, London, England, Board of Trade Papers, Georgia, Volume 27.

[19] Gipson, *British Empire,* VI, 290-291.

[20]*Ibid.,* VI, 291-293.

[21]*Ibid.,* VI, 292-293.

[22]*Ibid.,* VI, 293-295.

[23]*Ibid.,* VI, 294-295.

[24]"Mémoire sur les Acadiens," 1763, Canadian Archives, *Report* (1905), II, Appendix F, p. 151.

[25]Gipson, *British Empire,* VI, 295-297.

[26]Carl A. Brasseaux, "The Founding of New Acadia: Reconstruction and Transformation of Acadian Society in Louisiana, 1765-1865," 2 vols. (Thèse de doctorat, 3e cycle, Université de Paris, 1982), I, 90-91.

[27]John Thomas Scharf, *History of Maryland from Earliest Times to the Present Day,* 3 vols. (Baltimore, 1879), I, 476-477; Gregory A. Wood, *The French Presence in Maryland, 1524-1800* (Baltimore: 1978), p. 77; Basil Sollers, "The Acadians [French Neutrals] Transported to Maryland," *Maryland Historical Magazine,* III (1908), 14; *Maryland Gazette,* July 21, 1767.

[28]Brasseaux, "New Acadia," I, 95-96.

[29]*Ibid.,* I, 96-97.

[30]*Ibid.,* I, 97.

[31]*Ibid.*

[32]Sollers, "Acadians," 18; *Maryland Gazette,* February 10, 1757.

[33]Brasseaux, "New Acadia," 98-102.

[34]Wilton Paul Ledet, "Acadian Exiles in Pennsylvania," *Pennsylvania History,* X (1942), 120; *Pennsylvania Colonial Records: Minutes of the Provincial*

Council of Pennsylvania, 16 vols. (Philadelphia, 1838-1853), VI, 712.

[35]William Reed, "The French Neutrals in Pennsylvania," *Pennsylvania Historical Society Memoirs,* VI (1858), 298; *Colonial Records,* VI, 55-58.

[36]Gipson, *British Empire,* VI, 312; Reed, "French Neutrals," 298-300; Ledet, "Acadian Exiles," 122.

[37]Reed, "French Neutrals," 300.

[38]*Pennsylvania Archives: Votes and Proceedings of the House of Representatives of the Province of Pennsylvania, Eighth Series,* 8 vols. (Philadelphia, 1931-1935), VI, 4408; Ledet, "Acadian Exiles," 126.

[39]Ledet, "Acadian Exiles,"123; *Pennsylvania Archives,* VI, 4491-4492.

[40]*Pennsylvania Archives,* VI, 4509.

[41]The Acadian prisoners were Charles LeBlanc, Jean-Baptiste Galerme, Philippe Melancon, Paul Bijaud, and Jean Landry. Lord Loudoun to William Pitt, April 25, 1757, quoted in Gipson, *British Empire,* VI, 305.

[42]Brasseaux, "New Acadia," 114-118.

[43]Gipson, *British Empire,* VI, 319-320.

[44]*Ibid.,* 320-321.

[45]*Ibid.,* 321.

[46]*Ibid.,* 322-323.

[47]Lauvrière, *Tragédie,* II, 112, 116.

[48]Gipson, *British Empire,* VI, 325-326.

[49]*Ibid.,* 325.

[50]*Ibid.,* 326-327.

[51]*Ibid.,* 328-329.

[52]*Ibid.,* 329.

[53]*Ibid.,* 333-334; Michel Poirier, *Les Acadiens aux îles Saint-Pierre et Miquelon, 1758-1828* (Moncton, N.B., 1984), p. 22.

[54]Daigle, ed., *The Acadians of the Maritimes,* p. 159.

[55]Gipson, *British Empire,* VI, 334-336.

[56]For a history of Chéticamp, see Anselme Chiasson, *Chéticamp: Histoire et traditions acadiennes* (Moncton, N. B., 1961).

[57]Daigle, ed., *Acadians of the Maritimes*, p. 159.

[58]Under French rule the island was known as Ile St-Jean. The British christened it Prince Edward Island, a name which was officially applied to the island in 1799.

[59]See D. C. Harvey, *The French Regime in Prince Edward Island* (New Haven, 1926), pp. 175-238, suggests that there were 3,400 Acadians living on Prince Edward Island in 1758. A more recent study suggests that there may have been as many as 5,000 Acadians on Prince Edward Island in 1758. Daigle, ed., *Acadians of the Maritimes*, p. 161.

[60]In 1768, there were only sixty-eight English colonists on the island. *Ibid.*, p. 161.

[61]*Ibid.*

[62]*Ibid.*

[63]*Ibid.*; Henri Blanchard, *The Acadians of Prince Edward Island* (Ottawa, 1964), p. 70.

[64]William O. Raymond, *The River St. John: Its Physical Features, Legends and History from 1604 to 1784* (Sackville, N.B., 1950), pp. 96-101.

[65]A sailing vessel about the size of a brig.

[66]Raymond, *St. John*, pp. 105-107.

[67]*Ibid.*, pp. 110-114.

[68]*Ibid.*, pp. 116-119.

[69]Thomas Albert, *Histoire du Madawaska*, 2 vols. (Quebec, 1920), I, 70-71.

[70]*Ibid.*, I, 72-73; Raymond, *St. John.*, pp. 126-127.

[71]Ecoupag. This settlement included sixty-eight families, numbering "357 souls." Albert, *Madawaska*, I, 79.

[72]*Ibid.*, I, 75-114.

[73]*Ibid.*

[74]Quoted in Esther Clark Wright, *The Miramichi: A Study of the New Brunswick Riber and of the People Who Settled Along It* (Sackville, N. B., 1945), p. 15.

[75]On the fate of the Acadians who remained in the eastern Canada after 1755, see Brasseaux, *Founding*, pp. 20-30. See also Esther Clark Wright, *The Petitcodiac: A Study of the New Brunswick River and of the People Who Settled Along It* (Sackville, N.B., [1945]), pp. 14-15.

[76]Brasseaux, *Founding*, pp. 20-22. For information regarding a large privateer

operating along the northern New Brunswick coast, see William Francis Ganong, *The History of Caraquet and Pokemouche* (St. John, N. B., 1948), pp. 13-14.

[77]*Ibid.*

[78]Ganong, *Caraquet,* pp. 13-21.

[79]*Ibid.;* Daigle, ed., *Acadians of the Maritimes,* pp. 163-165.

[80]Ganong, *Caraquet,* p. 20.

[81]Gipson, *British Empire,* VI, 336-337; Lauvrière, *Tragédie,* II, 162, 258-259; Dorothy Vinter, "The Acadian Exiles in England," *Les Cahiers de la Société historique acadienne,* 30ieme cahier (1971), 388-402; Regis Godefroy Brun, "Le Sojourn des Acadiens en Angleterre et leurs traces dans les archives britanniques," *Les Cahiers de la Société historique acadienne,* 32ieme cahier (1971), 62-67.

[82]Oscar Winzerling, *Acadian Odyssey* (Baton Rouge, 1955), p. 39.

[83]See Choiseul to Hocquart, June 30,1763. AC, B 117:380vo.

[84]*Ibid.,* pp. 60-64.

[85]Brasseaux, *Founding,* pp. 55-64.

[86]*Ibid.,* pp. 64-65; Winzerling, *Acadian Odyssey,* pp. 76-79.

[87]Brasseaux, *Founding,* pp. 67-68.

[88]*Ibid.,* pp. 70-72; Winzerling, *Acadian Odyssey,* pp. 124-128; Milton P. Rieder, comp., *The Crew and Passenger Registration Lists of Seven Acadian Expeditions of 1785.* Metairie, La., 1965.

[89]W. J. Eccles, *France in America* (New York, 1972), pp. 217-218; Jacqueline K. Voorhies, "The Promised Land? The Acadians in the Antilles, 1763-1764," *Attakapas Gazette,* XI (1976), 81-83; C. A. Banbuck, *Histoire politique, économique et sociale de la Martinique sou l'ancien régime (1635-1789)* Paris, 1935), pp. 142-145.

[90]Voorhies, "Promised Land," 81.

[91]*Ibid.,* 82.

[92]Jonathan Brown, *The History and Present Condition of St. Domingo,* 2 vols., 2nd ed. (London, 1972), I, 115-116.

[93]Gabriel Debien, "The Acadians in Santo Domingo: 1764-1789," trans. by Glenn R. Conrad, in Glenn R. Conrad, ed., *The Cajuns: Essays on Their History and Culture* (Lafayette, La., 1978), p. 69.

[94]For the best biography of d'Estaing, see Jacques Michel, *La Vie aventureuse et*

mouvementée de Charles-Henri, comte d'Estaing (n.p., 1976).

[95]Voorhies, "Promised Land," 82-83.

[96]Michel, *Comte d'Estaing,* p. 113.

[97]Debien, "Santo Domingo," 29.

[98]*Ibid.,* p. 63.

[99]Shortly after their arrival at Môle Saint-Nicolas, numerous Acadian marriages were blessed and numerous baptisms were performed, leading Debien to conclude that these Acadians had formerly resided in the British seaboard colonies. *Ibid.,* 47.

[100]See Debien, "Santo Domingo," 31, note 19 for an explanation of the size of a *carreau.*

[101]A public works project in which all able-bodied men were expected to participate.

[102]Debien, "Santo Domingo," 31-32.

[103]*Ibid.,* pp. 73-78.

[104]*Ibid.,* pp. 32-40.

[105]*Ibid.,* pp. 54-55.

[106]*Ibid.,* pp. 60-61.

[107]*Ibid.,* p. 69.

[108]*Ibid.,* pp. 62-64.

[109]*Ibid.,* p. 65.

[110]Quoted in *ibid.,* pp. 68-70.

[111]*Ibid.,* pp. 75-77, 79.

[112]*Ibid.,* pp. 78-81.

[113]*Ibid.,* pp. 85-86.

[114]*Ibid.,* pp. 87-89.

[115]See, for example, *ibid.,* pp. 87, 92.

[116]*Ibid.,* pp. 89-92.

[117] Banbuck, *Histoire politique, économique et sociale de la Martinique,* for example, makes no mention of the Acadian immigrants.

[118]*Ibid.*, p. 25.

[119]*Ibid.*

[120]*Ibid.*, pp. 25-26.

[121]An island off the coast of French Guiana which had earlier been colonized by the French.

[122]Placide Gaudet, "Généalogies des Familles Acadiennes," *Report Concerning Canadian Archives for the Year 1905*, 2 vols. (Ottawa, 1905), II, 150; Poirier, *Acadiens*, p. 50.

[123]Lauvrière, *Tragédie*, II, 181-184.

[124]See Choiseul to Praslin, August 1, 1763. AC, B 117:435-435vo.

[125]According to the duc de Choiseul, the first wave consisted of 1,500 persons from St. Jean d'Angely, 180 from Thierry, and 100 members of the Karrer Regiment. Choiseul to Chanvallon, July 19, 1763. AC, B 117:415-415vo.

[126]Minister to Mistal, June 21, 1763. AC, B 117:358.

[127]Lauvrière, *Tragédie*, II, 185-186.

[128]Lauvrière, *Tragédie*, 184.

[129]*Ibid.*

[130]*Ibid.*, 186-187.

[131]See Julius Goebel, Jr., *The Struggle for the Falkland Islands: A Study in Legal and Diplomatic History* (1927; reprint ed., Port Washington, N.Y., 1927). The Falklands were called Iles Malouines by the French and Las Malvinas by the Spanish.

[132]See Minister to Bougainville, June 7, 1763. AC, B 117:330; Minister to the Comptroller General, June 7,1763. AC, B 117:331; Minister to Bougainville, June 21, 1763. AC, B 117:356.

[133]The expedition originally included three Acadian families. One family left the vessel after the male members refused to be pressed into service as part-time sailors. The unidentified family asked to be put ashore at St-Servan, near St. Malo, France; they were forced to debark instead at "Saint-Cast," a small village approximately ten miles west of St. Malo. "Des Acadiens aux Iles Falkland en 1763," *Les Cahiers de la Société Historique Acadienne*, VII (1976), 194-195; V. F. Boyson, *The Falkland Islands* (Oxford, 1924), p. 41.

[134]Minister to Bougainville, June 7, 1763. AC, B 117:330.

[135]Sometimes called Port Louis in English-language sources.

[136]Goebel, *The Struggle for the Falklands,* p. 226; Louis-Antoine de Bougainville, *A Voyage Round the World,* trans. by John Reinhold Forster, 2 vols. (London, 1772), I, 40; Minister to Praslin, August 7 1764. AC, B 120:344.

[137]Boyson, *The Falkland Islands,* p. 43.

[138]Minister to Guillot, August 6, 1764. AC, B 120:339-339vo.

[139]Lauvrière, *Tragédie,* II, 187-188; Hoffman and Hoffman, *Sovereignty in Dispute,* p. 40.

[140]Goebel, *The Struggle for the Falklands,* p. 226, 236.

[141]*Ibid.,* p. 239-240; Lauvrière, *Tragédie,* II, 188.

[142]Bougainville was paid 618,108 *livres,* 13 *sols,* and 11 *deniers.* Boyson, *The Falkland Islands,* p. 49.

[143]Bougainville, *Voyage,* I, 35; Goebel, *The Struggle for the Falklands,* p. 230.

[144]Boyson, *The Falkland Islands,* p. 51.

[145]Goebel, *The Struggle for the Falklands,* p. 230.

[146]Boyson, *The Falkland Islands,* p. 52.

[147]Bougainville left the Acadians a herd of seven heifers, two young bulls, eight sows, two boars, a few sheep, a kid, two horses and one mare.   After 1767, the Spanish colonial government reportedly introduced a small number of cattle. Left largely unsupervised, the cattle multiplied rapidly, and by 1785 there were 7,774 head of livestock on East Falkland. *Ibid.,* p. 195.

[148]*Ibid.,* pp. 53, 56, 59, 219.

[149]*Ibid.,* p. 79.

[150]Lauvrière, *Tragédie,* II, 189.

[151]*Ibid.,* II, 203-226.

[152]Poirier, *Acadiens,* pp. 19, 45.

[153]*Ibid.,* pp. 19-57; Lauvrière, *Tragédie,* II, 203-226.

[154]Dangeac was appointed governor on February 23, 1763. Poitier, *Acadiens,* p. 45.

[155]*Ibid.,* pp. 45-46.

[156]Dangeac indicates that the latter group, consisting of seventy-two individuals, had originally intended to sail from Beauséjour to Halifax aboard the *Polly and Jenny,* but when they were blown off course, the Acadians insisted that their captain put ashore at Miquelon to enable the passengers to visit relatives living there. After going ashore, the Acadians refused to board the vessel and return to

Nova Scotia, where they remained *persona non grata*. The captain, William Alan, who had not secured payment in advance, was forced to leave empty-handed. Poirier, *Acadiens*, pp. 53-54.

[157]Lauvrière, *Tragédie*, II, 206.

[158]Poirier, *Acadiens*, pp. 46, 51, 69. Many of the Acadians sent to Nantes soon died of smallpox.

[159]*Ibid.*, pp. 53-55.

[160]Quoted in Lauvrière, *Tragédie*, II, 209.

[161]Poirier, *Acadians*, p. 87.

[162]Poirier, *Acadiens*, p. 30; Lauvrière, *Tragédie*, II, 208, 210. J. S. Bourinot claimed that "300 to 400" Acadians migrated from Miquelon to Cape Breton and the Iles Madame "after 1766." Other statistics sited by this historian are at variance from those used by more recent writers. See J. S. Bourinot, Cape Breton and Its Memorials, 2 vols. (Ottawa, 1891), II, 173-342.

[163]Lauvrière, *Tragédie*, II, 210-213.

[164]Approximately 100 Acadians remained at Rochefort, France. Poirier, *Acadiens*, pp. 86-93.

[165]*Ibid.*, p. 94.

[166]*Ibid.*

[167]*Ibid.*, p. 95.

[168]Miquelon had a population of 776 persons, while St. Pierre supported 1,028 inhabitants. Some of the foregoing inhabitants were itinerant fishermen, migrating from France to the islands during the cod season; approximately sixty-five percent of the population, however was sedentary. Most of the permanent residents (fifty-six percent) made their homes on Miquelon island. *Ibid.*, p. 96.

[169]The declaration of war marked France's entrance into the American Revolution as an American ally.

[170]Poirier, *Acadiens*, p. 98.

[171]*Ibid.*, pp. 101-103.

[172]*Ibid*, p. 123.

[173]Lauvrière, *Tragédie*, II, 221-222.

[174]*Ibid.*, p. 222.

[175]Poirier, *Acadiens*, pp. 124-125.

[176]Poirier, *Acadiens,* pp. 171-173.

[177]See LeBlanc, "The Acadian Migrations," pp. 55-59.

[178]Brasseaux, "New Acadia," pp. 158, 205-06.

[179]Jacqueline K. Voorhies, comp., *Some Late Eighteenth Century Louisianians* (Lafayette, La., 1973), pp. 114-119; Jehn, comp., *Acadian Exiles in the Colonies* .

[180]There were initially 193 Acadian immigrants, but by April 1765, their number had grown to 231. Denis-Nicolas Foucault to Minister of Marine Choiseul, Feb. 28, 1765. Archives Nationales, Paris, France, Archives des Colonies (hereinafter AC), subseries C 13a (Louisiane: correspondance générale), volume 45, folio 12.

[181]Gabriel Debien, "Les Acadiens a Saint-Domingue," in Glenn R. Conrad, ed., *The Cajuns: Essays on Their History and Culture* (Lafayette, La., 1978), p. 262.

[182]Brasseaux, "New Acadia," pp. 71-74.

[183]Akins, ed., *Acadia and Nova Scotia,* pp. 349-350.

[184]*Ibid.*

[185]Brasseaux, "New Acadia," p. 159.

[186]Foucault to Choiseul, Feb. 25, 1765. AC, C 13a, vol. 45, folio 42.

[187]Carl A. Brasseaux, *"L'Officier de Plume:* Denis-Nicolas Foucault, *commissaire-ordonnateur* of French Louisiana, 1762-1769" (M.A. thesis, University of Southwestern Louisiana, 1975), pp. 27, 37, 61, 62, 64.

[188]List of provisions and supplies delivered to the Acadian families who have taken refuge in Louisiana, Apr. 30, 1765. AC, C 13a, vol. 45, folio 30; Charles Philippe Aubry and Foucault to Choiseul, Apr. 30, 1765. AC, C 13a. 45:21-24; Jacqueline K. Voorhies, trans., "The Attakapas Post: The First Acadian Settlement," *Louisiana History,* XVII (1976), 91-96.

[189]"Copie d'un vieux registre de St. Martin de Tours" (typescript of the oldest church registers, St. Martin de Tours Catholic Church, St. Martinville, Louisiana), pp. 1-3; Attakapas General Census, Oct. 30, 1774, Archivo National de Indies, Seville, Spain, Papeles Procedentes de Cuba (hereinafter PPC), legajo 218.

[190]Antonio de Ulloa to Jeronimo de Grimaldi, May 19, 1766, Archivo General de Indias, Seville, Spain, Audiencia de Santo Domingue (hereinafter ASD), legajo 2585, non paginated.

[191]Henry Jerningham to Ulloa, Nov. 1766, in Lawrence Kinnard, ed., *Spain in the Mississippi Valley, 1765-1794,* 3 vols. (Washington, D. C., 1946), II, 36-7.

[192]Ulloa to Grimaldi, Sept. 29, 1766, ASD, 2585:n.p.; Aubry to Ulloa, Dec. 16, 1766, legajo 187A, non-paginated, PPC; Richard E. Chandler, trans. and ed., "End of

an Odyssey: Acadians Arrive in St. Gabriel, Louisiana," *Louisiana History,* XIV (1973), 81-7; Ulloa to Grimaldi, July 23, 1767, legajo 2585, n.p., ASD; Pedro Piernas to Ulloa, June 5, 1767, legajo 187A:n.p, PPC.

[193]Ulloa to Grimaldi, May 19, 1766, ASD, legajo 2585:n.p.

[194] *Ibid.*

[195]*Ibid.*

[196]Richard E. Chandler, trans. and ed., "Odyssey Continued: Acadians Arrive in Natchez," *Louisiana History,* XIX (1978), 447; Chandler, trans. and ed., "End of an Odyssey," 81-87.

[197]Ulloa, "Observations," 1769. AC, C 13a, vol. 47, folios 121-121vo.

[198]David Ker Texada, *Alejandro O'Reilly and the New Orleans Rebels* (Lafayette, La., 1970), pp. 88-89.

[199]Carl A. Brasseaux and Richard E. Chandler, "The Britain Incident, 1769-1770: Anglo-Hispanic Tensions in the Western Gulf," *Southwestern Quarterly,* LXXXVII (1984), 357-370; Carl A. Brasseaux, "The Long Road to Louisiana: Acadian Exiles and the *Britain* Incident," *Gulf Coast Historical Review,* I (1985), 24-38.

[200]Minister of Marine Praslin to Mistral, Sept. 13, 1766. Archives Nationales, Paris, France, Archives des Colonies, Subseries B (ordres du roi), volume 125, folio 450vo.

[201]Memoir on Acadian History to 1778, June 1778. Archives Nationales, Paris, France, Archives des Affaires etrangères, Angleterre subseries, volume 47, folio 23.

[202]Praslin to Mistral, Sept. 13, 1766. AC, B 125:450vo.

[203]Mathé Allain, trans., "The Records of Belle-Isle-en-Mer," *Attakapas Gazette,* XVI (1981), 103-110; XVII (1982), 36-45, 76-83, 123-131, 183-192; XVIII (1983), 73-80, 108-113.

[204]On the 1785 Acadian migration to Louisiana, see Oscar W. Winzerling, *Acadian Odyssey* (Baton Rouge, La., 1955).

[205]Brasseaux, "New Acadia," p. 215.

[206]*Ibid.*

[207]Anselme Blanchard to Carondelet, Oct. 28, 1794, PPC, 209:356.

[208]Historian Gabriel Debien, for example, makes no distinction between natives of Saint-Domingue and the transplanted Acadian exiles in his landmark articles on the Saint-Domingue refugees: "Les Colons de Saint-Domingue Réfugiés à Cuba (1793-1815)," *Revista de Indias,* XIII (1953), 559-605; XIV (1954), 11-36.

Index

82